AMERICA'S —
TEST KITCHEN

Kitchen Explorers!

Library of Congress Cataloging-in-Publication Data has been applied for.

ISBN 9781948703628

America's Test Kitchen

21 Drydock Avenue, Boston, MA 02210

Manufactured in the United States of America
10 9 8 7 6 5 4 3 2 1

Distributed by Penguin Random House Publisher Services
Tel: 800.733.3000

Editor in Chief: Molly Birnbaum

Executive Food Editor: Suzannah McFerran

Deputy Editor, Education: Kristin Sargianis

Senior Editor: Afton Cyrus

Test Cook: Andrea Wawrzyn

Assistant Editor: Katy O'Hara

Creative Director: John Torres

Designer: Sarah Horwitch Dailey

Illustrator: Gabi Homonoff

Silly Story Writer: Chad Chenail

Senior Manager, Publishing Operations: Taylor Argenzio

Copy Editors: Christine Campbell, April Poole, Rachel Schowalter

Chief Creative Officer: Jack Bishop

Executive Editorial Directors: Julia Collin Davison, Bridget Lancaster

Table of Contents

Introduction

Welcome to *Kitchen Explorers!* We created this workbook to help you learn to cook, nerd out with science using food, and, more importantly, have fun.

The recipes, experiments, and activities in this workbook are all kid-tested and kid-approved. This means that our group of more than 8,000 volunteer kid testers from around the country have cooked all the recipes and done all the experiments and activities you'll find on the pages ahead—giving us suggestions and feedback along the way—and they would make them again or recommend them to their friends.

This workbook is for you to write in, draw in, and make completely your own. Food is a wonderful way to get creative, to get messy, and to learn. You'll probably make some mistakes, but that's OK (they will still be delicious). Be proud of all that you accomplish!

More than 8,000 kids helped create this book!

READY, SET, GO!

Understanding the Symbols in This Workbook

To help you find the right recipe, experiment, or activity for you, we use a system of symbols to quickly show the type of cooking required:

 = requires use of knife

= requires use of microwave

= requires use of stovetop

= requires use of oven

= no knives or heat required

Rate Your Recipes

As you make each recipe, take notes (or make drawings) on the page. When you're finished, rate the recipe! Pick the emoji that best describes what you thought of the recipe and circle it or color it in.

How to Read the Recipes in This Workbook

Cooking from a recipe is actually a three-step process, and the recipes in this workbook are written to reflect that, with three distinct sections. Bonus: Each recipe is accompanied by additional information or activities to grow your food and cooking knowledge.

Prepare Ingredients

Start with the list of ingredients and prepare them as directed. Measure ingredients, melt butter, and chop ingredients as needed. Wash fruits and vegetables. You can use small prep bowls to keep ingredients organized.

Gather Cooking Equipment

Once all your ingredients are ready, put all the tools you will need to follow the recipe instructions on the counter.

Start Cooking

It's finally time to start cooking. Any ingredients that need to be prepped at the last minute will have instructions within the recipe itself. Don't forget to have fun!

Food for Thought

Food and cooking are about SO MUCH more than just what's happening in your pot or pan or bowl. Each recipe has a special "Food for Thought" section to inspire you to expand your knowledge and learn something new!

Kitchen Math

You can get carried away learning all the math behind measuring. Memorize the following rules and you will be all set.

3 teaspoons	=	1 tablespoon
16 tablespoons	=	1 cup
16 ounces	=	1 pound
2 cups	=	1 pint
4 cups	=	1 quart
4 quarts	=	1 gallon

Kitchen Safety Tips

- Wash your hands before cooking and after touching raw meat or eggs.
- Knives and stoves can be dangerous. Always ask for help if you're in doubt.
- Assume that anything on the stove or in the oven is hot. Use oven mitts.
- Never let ingredients you eat raw (such as berries) touch foods you will cook (such as eggs).
- Always turn off the stovetop and oven when you're done cooking.

How to Read the Experiments in This Workbook

The goal of an experiment is to answer a question—such as "What's the difference between baking powder and baking soda?" or "How do bubbles get into fizzy beverages?"—by gathering data and analyzing it. Like recipes, experiments follow a step-by-step process.

Materials

Start with the list of materials and prepare them as directed. Sometimes these materials are ingredients and kitchen equipment, but, depending on the experiment, they might include other materials from around your house, such as craft materials or art supplies.

Make a Prediction

Before beginning an experiment, scientists use what they already know to make a prediction—an educated guess—about the answer to the question they're exploring. It helps them (and you!) think through the possibilities and record their ideas.

Observe Your Results

Now on to the testing! When you conduct your experiment following the steps in this book, carefully observe the results—there are designated spaces to write down (or draw pictures of) what you notice happening! Do your observations support or disprove your prediction? In this book, you'll use all your senses—sight, touch, taste, smell, and hearing—as you make your observations.

Understanding Your Results

After (and only after!) you've finished your experiment, read an explanation of the science behind your observations and learn more about the results we got when we did these experiments in the America's Test Kitchen Kids lab.

Decoding Kitchenspeak

Reading a recipe can sometimes feel like reading a foreign language. Here are some common words in many recipes and what they really mean.

PEEL: To remove the outer skin, rind, or layer from food, usually a piece of fruit or a vegetable. Often done with a vegetable peeler.

ZEST: To remove the flavorful colored outer peel from a citrus fruit such as a lemon, lime, or orange (the colored skin is called the zest). Does not include the bitter white layer (called the pith) under the zest.

CHOP: To cut food with a knife into small pieces. Chopped fine = ⅛- to ¼-inch pieces. Chopped = ¼- to ½-inch pieces. Chopped coarse = ½- to ¾-inch pieces. Use a ruler to understand the different sizes.

SLICE: To cut food with a knife into pieces with two flat sides, with the thickness dependent on the recipe instructions. For example, slicing a celery stalk.

GRATE: To cut food (often cheese) into very small, uniform pieces using a rasp grater or the small holes on a box grater.

STIR: To combine ingredients in a bowl or cooking vessel, often with a rubber spatula or wooden spoon.

TOSS: To gently combine ingredients with tongs or two forks and/or spoons in order to distribute the ingredients evenly. You toss salad in a bowl (you don't stir it).

MELT: To heat solid food (think butter) on the stovetop or in the microwave until it becomes a liquid.

SIMMER: To heat liquid until small bubbles gently break the surface at a variable and infrequent rate, as when cooking a soup.

BOIL: To heat liquid until large bubbles break the surface at a rapid and constant rate, as when cooking pasta.

Decoding Experimentspeak

Reading a science experiment can sometimes feel like reading a foreign language, too! Here are some common words in many experiments and what they really mean.

PREDICTION: An educated guess, based on your knowledge and experience, about what will happen in an experiment.

OBSERVATION: The act of careful watching, listening, touching, tasting, or smelling. When conducting experiments, scientists record their observations, usually by writing, drawing, or taking photos.

SUBJECT: When scientists conduct experiments, their "subjects" are the people whose reactions or responses they're studying.

VARIABLE: Something that can be changed. In experiments, scientists change at least one variable to observe what happens.

Here's an example: Scientists are studying whether the type of sugar affects the flavor and texture of cookies. They add brown sugar to one batch of cookies and white sugar to a second batch of cookies. The type of sugar is the variable.

CONTROLS: The variables that are not changed in an experiment.

For example, when the scientists are studying whether the type of sugar affects the flavor and texture of cookies, they use the same types and amounts of all cookie ingredients (except the sugar) and bake the cookies at the same temperature for the same amount of time.

BLIND: When the subjects of the experiment do not know what is being tested.

For example, subjects might wear a blindfold when tasting two different foods so that they can't see what they're eating, or they might taste two batches of pasta, one cooked with salt and one cooked without salt, without being told what is different about them.

RESULTS: What happens in an experiment, usually a combination of the observations and measurements recorded and interpreted by scientists.

Sketch All of these recipes were developed in our test kitchen. Draw what you think the test kitchen looks like in the box below!

CHAPTER 1 Recipes and Make It Your Way Challenges

Yogurt Parfaits

 SERVES 2
TOTAL TIME 15 minutes

Greek yogurt makes the creamiest parfait, but you can use regular plain yogurt instead. Regular yogurt is thinner than Greek yogurt (extra liquid has been drained from Greek yogurt so that it's really thick and creamy), so the layers may not stay as well defined.

Prepare Ingredients

1 cup plain Greek yogurt

1 tablespoon honey

1 cup raspberries, blueberries, blackberries, and/or sliced strawberries

½ cup granola

Gather Cooking Equipment

Small bowl

Whisk

Spoon

Two 8-ounce glasses

¼-cup dry measuring cup

1-tablespoon measuring spoon

Start Cooking!

1 In small bowl, whisk yogurt and honey until smooth. Spoon one-quarter of the yogurt-honey mixture into each glass. Top with ¼ cup berries, followed by 2 tablespoons granola.

2 Repeat layering process with remaining yogurt-honey mixture, berries, and granola. When you're done, you should have 2 layers each of yogurt-honey mixture, berries, and granola. Serve within 15 minutes or granola will start to become soggy.

Notes Use this space to write what you liked (or didn't like) about this recipe or draw a picture of what you made!

Food for Thought

What makes Greek yogurt different from regular yogurt? Let's find out!

If you've got some regular plain yogurt and some plain Greek yogurt in your refrigerator, conduct a taste test. Observe both varieties, stir them with a spoon, and take a taste. What do you notice about each type of yogurt? What's its texture like? Its flavor?

Greek yogurt is made the same way that regular yogurt is made—just with an extra step at the end: Greek yogurt is strained for several hours, usually in cheesecloth (a woven fabric with holes in it). As the yogurt sits in the cheesecloth, a clear liquid called whey (pronounced "way") drains out. This makes Greek yogurt thicker and creamier than regular yogurt. Whey is made of water and proteins (called whey proteins)—not to worry, though, there are still plenty of proteins in the Greek yogurt that's left behind.

You can try making your own Greek yogurt at home! Here's how to do it.

1 Line fine-mesh strainer with 2 layers of cheesecloth or 3 basket-style coffee filters. Set strainer inside medium bowl.

2 Add regular yogurt to cheesecloth-lined strainer. Cover strainer and bowl with plastic wrap and place in refrigerator for at least 8 hours or up to 24 hours.

3 Remove strainer and bowl from refrigerator. Transfer Greek yogurt from strainer to an airtight container and store in the refrigerator for up to 1 week.

4 Try a taste test! Eat some of your Greek yogurt (you can taste the whey, too!). What do you notice about its flavor? Its texture? How is it different from regular yogurt? How is it the same?

Do not use yogurt containing modified food starch, gelatin, or ingredients called "gums" for this activity.

Strawberry-Peach Smoothies

 SERVES 2
TOTAL TIME 10 minutes

Colorful, creamy, and supersmooth—these smoothies will make a fruity part of your breakfast, lunch, or snack!

Prepare Ingredients

1 ripe banana, peeled and broken into 4 pieces

1 tablespoon honey

1 cup frozen strawberries

1 cup frozen peaches

1 cup plain yogurt

¼ cup orange juice

Gather Cooking Equipment

Blender

Dish towel

Rubber spatula

2 glasses

Start Cooking!

1 Place banana and honey in blender. Put lid on top of blender and hold lid firmly in place with folded dish towel. Process until smooth, about 10 seconds.

2 Stop blender. Add strawberries, peaches, yogurt, and orange juice. Replace lid and process for 30 seconds. Stop blender and scrape down sides of blender jar with rubber spatula.

3 Replace lid and continue to process until smooth, about 30 seconds longer. Pour into glasses and serve.

Notes
Use this space to write what you liked (or didn't like) about this recipe or draw a picture of what you made!

Once you master smoothie basics, the combinations are endless. Frozen fruit keeps things cold. If you have fresh fruit, place it in the freezer before you go to bed—voilà, frozen fruit.

Primary Colors

Red   Yellow   Blue

Secondary Colors: Make by mixing two primary colors

Red + Yellow = Orange   Red + Blue = Purple   Yellow + Blue = Green

Write the color of each smoothie ingredient here. Are they primary or secondary colors?

Based on the colors of your ingredients, what color do you predict your smoothie will be?

Blueberry Muffins

MAKES 12 muffins

TOTAL TIME 55 minutes, plus cooling time

If using frozen berries, do not thaw.

Prepare Ingredients

Vegetable oil spray

3 cups (15 ounces) plus 1 tablespoon all-purpose flour, measured separately

1 cup (7 ounces) sugar

1 tablespoon baking powder

½ teaspoon baking soda

½ teaspoon salt

1½ cups plain yogurt

2 large eggs

8 tablespoons unsalted butter, melted and cooled

1½ cups fresh or frozen blueberries

Gather Cooking Equipment

12-cup muffin tin

3 bowls (1 large, 1 medium, 1 small)

Whisk

Rubber spatula

⅓-cup dry measuring cup

Toothpick

Oven mitts

Cooling rack

Start Cooking!

1 Adjust oven rack to middle position and heat oven to 375 degrees. Spray 12-cup muffin tin with vegetable oil spray.

2 In large bowl, whisk together 3 cups flour, sugar, baking powder, baking soda, and salt. In medium bowl, whisk yogurt and eggs until smooth.

3 Add yogurt mixture to large bowl with flour mixture and use rubber spatula to stir gently until just combined and no dry flour is visible. Gently stir in melted butter.

4 In small bowl, toss blueberries with remaining 1 tablespoon flour. Gently stir blueberries into batter. Do not overmix.

5 Use ⅓-cup dry measuring cup to divide batter evenly among muffin cups.

6 Place muffin tin in oven and bake until golden brown and toothpick inserted in center of muffin comes out clean, 20 to 25 minutes.

7 Use oven mitts to remove muffin tin from oven (ask an adult for help). Place muffin tin on cooling rack and let muffins cool in tin for 15 minutes.

8 Using your fingertips, gently wiggle muffins to loosen from muffin tin and transfer to cooling rack. Let cool for at least 10 minutes before serving.

Notes Use this space to write what you liked (or didn't like) about this recipe or draw a picture of what you made!

Food for Thought

Blueberries are *berries* . . . right?! Well, hold on. Before we say yes or no, let's do some investigation. Start by setting aside a few extra blueberries before you start cooking. When the muffins are baking in step 6, take a moment to observe those extra blueberries. What do they look like? Draw a picture, or take some notes.

Next, cut them in half across their equator (or ask an adult for help) and take a look at their insides. Do you see any seeds? Draw what you see.

These seeds are a key clue as to whether these berries are *actually* berries! Because raspberries, strawberries, and blackberries AREN'T ACTUALLY BERRIES. (Well, at least according to plant scientists they aren't.) But blueberries are. (Phew!)

In our everyday conversations, "berries" are small fruits that grow on a bush. But, if you ask a plant scientist "What's a berry?" they will give you a different answer: A berry is a fruit that grows from one flower and usually contains several seeds inside. Blueberries fit this scientific definition, so scientists call them "true berries." But a single raspberry is actually made up of lots of tiny, round fruits, each with its own seed inside. Strawberries also contain many teeny individual fruits, each with their own yellow seed on the outside.

According to plant scientists, fruits such as bananas, kiwis, grapes, and even watermelons are berries, too! Each of these berries grows from its own flower and their sweet flesh surrounds tiny seeds.

Real Buttered Popcorn

 SERVES 3 to 4 (Makes 6 cups)
TOTAL TIME 15 minutes

Make sure to use a plain bag without any writing (colored inks are often not microwave-safe).

Prepare Ingredients

¼ cup popcorn kernels

½ teaspoon vegetable oil

1 tablespoon unsalted butter

¼ teaspoon salt

Gather Cooking Equipment

Clean brown paper lunch bag

Large microwave-safe plate

Oven mitts

Large microwave-safe bowl

Rubber spatula

Start Cooking!

1 Place popcorn kernels in clean brown paper lunch bag. Drizzle kernels with oil. Fold over top of bag three times to seal (do not tape or staple).

2 Shake bag to coat kernels with oil, place bag on its side on large microwave-safe plate, and shake kernels into even layer in bag.

3 Place plate in microwave and cook until popping slows down to 1 or 2 pops at a time, 3 to 5 minutes. Use oven mitts to remove plate from microwave (plate will be very hot, ask an adult for help). Set aside to cool slightly.

4 Place butter in large microwave-safe bowl (big enough to hold popcorn), cover, and heat in microwave at 50 percent power until melted, 30 to 60 seconds. Use oven mitts to remove bowl from microwave.

5 Carefully open paper bag (be careful, there will be hot steam) and pour popcorn into bowl with melted butter. Use rubber spatula to toss popcorn with butter. Sprinkle with salt. Serve.

Notes
Use this space to write what you liked (or didn't like) about this recipe or draw a picture of what you made!

"Pop" Quiz

Did you know that popped popcorn kernels can be different shapes?

The popcorn industry categorizes popped kernels into three basic shapes: **unilateral** (pieces that expand in one direction), **bilateral** (pieces that expand in two directions), and **multilateral** (pieces that expand in three or more directions). The crunchiest popcorns have more unilateral pieces. Take a look at the popcorn you made. What shapes do you see?

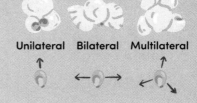

Unilateral   Bilateral   Multilateral

Food for Thought

Did you know that Americans consume 13 *billion* quarts of popcorn annually (enough to fill almost 5,000 Olympic-size swimming pools!)? But where does popcorn come from? And what makes popcorn pop?

Popcorn is made from corn, but not the same corn that we eat as corn on the cob—that's called sweet corn. Instead, popcorn is a different variety of corn called . . . POPCORN!

As for the popping, it all starts with dried popcorn kernels. The kernel has three main parts: the **hull**, which is like a hard shell; the

germ, which is what a new corn plant would grow from; and the **endosperm**, which is made of starch, tiny droplets of water, and a little bit of protein. The water in the endosperm is what puts the POP in popcorn.

As the kernels heat up, the starch in the endosperm gets softer and the tiny droplets of water expand and turn into steam. When enough steam builds up inside the kernel—at around 350 degrees—the hull breaks and the kernel explodes and turns inside-out! The starch and protein on the inside burst through the hull and turn solid in the cooler air, forming the white-yellow, pillowy part of popcorn kernels.

Tortilla Snack Chips

SERVES 4
TOTAL TIME 30 minutes

You can eat these chips on their own or with your favorite dips, such as hummus, guacamole, or salsa!

Prepare Ingredients

4 (8-inch) flour tortillas

Vegetable oil spray

½ teaspoon salt

Gather Cooking Equipment

Cutting board

Chef's knife

Large bowl

2 rimmed baking sheets

Oven mitts

2 cooling racks

Start Cooking!

1 Adjust oven racks to upper-middle and lower-middle positions and heat oven to 350 degrees.

2 Cut each tortilla into 8 wedges and transfer to large bowl. Spray wedges generously with vegetable oil spray. Sprinkle with salt. Use your hands to gently toss tortilla pieces until evenly coated on all sides. Use more cooking spray if needed.

3 Spread half of tortilla pieces onto rimmed baking sheet in single layer. Spread remaining tortilla pieces onto second rimmed baking sheet in single layer.

4 Place both baking sheets in oven and bake until chips are golden and crisp, 10 to 15 minutes. (Note that chips on lower rack may cook more quickly.)

5 Use oven mitts to remove baking sheets from oven (ask an adult for help). Place baking sheets on cooling racks and let chips cool for 10 minutes. Serve.

Notes Use this space to write what you liked (or didn't like) about this recipe or draw a picture of what you made!

Food for Thought

In step 2 of this recipe, you need to cut the round tortillas into 8 equal wedges. Making the wedges the same size helps the chips bake evenly.

Which tortilla below is divided into 8 **equal** wedges? Circle your answer.

While your tortilla chips bake, solve these tortilla fraction problems:

Color in ½ of the   Color in ¼ of the   Color in ⅜ of the
tortilla below: tortilla below: tortilla below:

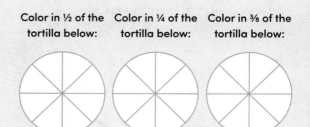

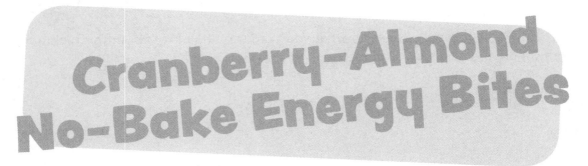

Cranberry-Almond No-Bake Energy Bites

 MAKES 12 bites
TOTAL TIME 15 minutes, plus 30 minutes chilling time

You can add 1 tablespoon of chia seeds or ground flaxseed to oat mixture in step 1, if desired.

Prepare Ingredients

¾ cup (2¼ ounces) old-fashioned rolled oats

⅓ cup creamy peanut, almond, or sunflower butter

⅓ cup sliced almonds

⅓ cup dried cranberries

2 tablespoons honey

⅛ teaspoon salt

Gather Cooking Equipment

Large bowl

Rubber spatula

1-tablespoon measuring spoon

Plate

Plastic wrap

Start Cooking!

1 In large bowl, combine all ingredients. Use rubber spatula to stir until well combined.

2 Use your wet hands to roll mixture into 12 balls (about 1 tablespoon each). Place balls on plate and cover with plastic wrap.

3 Place plate in refrigerator and chill until balls are firm, at least 30 minutes. Serve.

Notes Use this space to write what you liked (or didn't like) about this recipe or draw a picture of what you made!

Food for Thought

Chefs are great at cooking food, of course. But many are also good at *talking* about food—what it tastes like, smells like, feels like, and looks like—not always an easy task! Describing food is a skill that needs practice, and a LOT of words. Use this recipe as a chance to practice using your food vocabulary. As you measure, stir, and roll, observe what each ingredient looks like (its appearance) and feels like (its texture). Then, as you taste your finished energy bites, think about their appearance and texture. Write your observations in the spaces below. We added some examples for inspiration.

OATS	coarse
PEANUT BUTTER	sticky
SLICED ALMONDS	flat
DRIED CRANBERRIES	red
HONEY	translucent
SALT	tiny
ENERGY BITES	round

Simple Syrup

MAKES 1 cup
TOTAL TIME 10 minutes for plain simple syrup, 40 minutes for flavored syrups

Adding sweetness and flavor to drinks couldn't be "simpler" when you use this syrup! Make sure to use a jar that will still have some extra room in it after adding the water and sugar—you need space for the liquid to move around as you shake the jar. A pint- or quart-size jar works well.

Prepare Ingredients

⅔ cup sugar

⅔ cup water

1 flavor ingredient below (optional)
- 1 teaspoon grated lime zest plus 1 tablespoon juice
- 1 cup raspberries
- 1 cup quartered strawberries
- ½ cup pineapple chunks
- 1 cup mint leaves
- ½ cup chopped fresh ginger

Gather Cooking Equipment

Jar with tight-fitting lid

Fine-mesh strainer

Medium bowl

Start Cooking!

1 In jar, combine sugar, water, and flavor ingredient, if using. Cover jar with lid to seal. Shake jar vigorously until sugar dissolves, about 2 minutes.

2 Let jar sit on counter until syrup turns clear, about 5 minutes. (If making a flavored syrup, let jar sit on counter for 30 minutes to infuse flavor.)

3 If making flavored syrup, place fine-mesh strainer over bowl. Remove lid from jar and pour syrup mixture through fine-mesh strainer. Discard solids in strainer. Pour flavored syrup back into jar. (Simple syrup can be refrigerated for up to 1 month.)

Notes Use this space to write what you liked (or didn't like) about this recipe or draw a picture of what you made!

> I like to put on my favorite tunes and turn simple syrup shaking into a dance party!

Food for Thought

This recipe uses two ingredients—sugar and water—that happen to be in two different states of matter. Matter is anything that takes up space. Our whole world is made of matter—people, animals, the ocean, food, air, houses, rocks, everything! Matter can exist in three different states: solid, liquid, or gas. Solids keep their shape, even if they move around. Bananas, elephants, and plates are solids—and so is sugar! The tiny sugar crystals keep their own shapes as they move around. Liquids don't have their own shape; they take the shape of whatever container they're in. Water, maple syrup, and shampoo are all liquids.

Is your Simple Syrup a solid or a liquid?

Look around your kitchen: Can you find other examples of solids and liquids? Write or draw what you find in the spaces below.

Solids	Liquids

Flavored Seltzer

SERVES 1 (makes 1 cup)
TOTAL TIME 45 minutes (including making Flavored Syrup)

If you're making flavored seltzers for friends and family, mix them one glass at a time. A big batch needs a lot more stirring, which means you'll lose those bubbles!

Prepare Ingredients

Ice

1 cup plain seltzer

1 tablespoon Flavored Syrup (see Simple Syrup recipe, page 24)

Gather Cooking Equipment

Glass

Spoon

Start Cooking!

Place ice in glass. Pour plain seltzer into glass over ice. Add Flavored Syrup and stir gently to combine. Serve.

Try it THIS Way!

Flavored Seltzer Combos Once you master the flavored syrups basics, play around with different flavor combinations. Try shaking up a few different flavored syrups (see the Simple Syrup recipe on page 24 for flavor ideas), and then mix and match them! Here are three of our favorite combinations.

STRAWBERRY-MINT SELTZER Use 2 teaspoons Mint Syrup and 1 teaspoon Strawberry Syrup per 1 cup of plain seltzer.

PINEAPPLE-LIME SELTZER Use 2 teaspoons Pineapple Syrup and 1 teaspoon Lime Syrup per 1 cup of plain seltzer.

RASPBERRY-GINGER SELTZER Use 1½ teaspoons Raspberry Syrup and 1½ teaspoons Ginger Syrup per 1 cup of plain seltzer.

Notes Use this space to write what you liked (or didn't like) about this recipe or draw a picture of what you made!

Pesto Flatbread "Pizza"

SERVES 1 to 2
TOTAL TIME 40 minutes

Prepare Ingredients

1 teaspoon extra-virgin olive oil

1 (8-inch) naan bread

2 tablespoons pesto

⅓ cup shredded mozzarella cheese

12 cherry tomatoes, cut in half

Gather Cooking Equipment

Pastry brush

Ruler

Rimmed baking sheet

Small spoon

Oven mitts

Cooling rack

Spatula

Cutting board

Chef's knife or pizza wheel

Start Cooking!

1 Adjust oven rack to lowest position and heat oven to 400 degrees. Use pastry brush to brush oil into 9-inch circle in center of rimmed baking sheet. Place naan on top of oil.

2 Use back of small spoon to spread pesto over naan, leaving ½-inch border around edge. Sprinkle cheese over pesto, then scatter tomatoes over cheese.

3 Place baking sheet in oven and bake until naan is golden brown around edges, 8 to 10 minutes.

4 Use oven mitts to remove baking sheet from oven (ask an adult for help). Place baking sheet on cooling rack and let cool for 5 minutes.

5 Use spatula to carefully transfer naan to cutting board (baking sheet will be hot). Use chef's knife or pizza wheel to cut naan into wedges. Serve.

Notes Use this space to write what you liked (or didn't like) about this recipe or draw a picture of what you made!

Food for Thought

Did you know that quick-cooking flatbreads, such as naan, are the oldest breads in the world? Humans have been making and eating flatbreads for thousands and thousands of years, since the late Stone Age.

Today, many cultures around the world have their own unique flatbread recipes. Here are a few flatbreads from across the globe. How many have you heard of? Have you eaten any of them? See if you can find each country or region on a world map.

Naan (India) Naan is a chewy flatbread that's often eaten with stews and curries. It's traditionally cooked on the hot surface of a special tandoor oven.

Tortillas (Mexico) Tortillas can be made from corn or wheat and are used in tacos, tostadas, enchiladas, and more.

Lavash (Armenia) Lavash is a soft, thin flatbread that's usually rectangular. It can be rolled around fillings or baked into crisp crackers.

Pita (Middle East) People have been baking soft, tender pita bread—with its signature pocket—for thousands of years.

Injera (Ethiopia) Injera is a spongy flatbread made from a grain called teff. In Ethiopia, many dishes are served right on top of injera and people use pieces of the bread to pick up their food.

Fry Bread (North America, Native American) Fry Bread is a round, bubbly, fried dough (though different Native American tribes make different styles).

Meatballs

 SERVES 4 (Makes 12 meatballs)
TOTAL TIME 45 minutes

This recipe makes enough sauce to coat 12 ounces of pasta.

Prepare Ingredients

½ cup panko bread crumbs

½ cup milk

1 (28-ounce) can crushed tomatoes, opened

1 tablespoon extra-virgin olive oil

¼ teaspoon sugar

¼ teaspoon plus ½ teaspoon salt, measured separately

1 pound 85 percent lean ground beef

½ cup grated Parmesan cheese

½ teaspoon garlic powder

½ teaspoon dried oregano

Gather Cooking Equipment

Large bowl

Rubber spatula

Dutch oven with lid

1-tablespoon measuring spoon

Large plate

Start Cooking!

1　In large bowl, add panko and milk. Use rubber spatula to stir to combine. Let mixture sit for 5 minutes.

2　In Dutch oven, combine tomatoes, oil, sugar, and ¼ teaspoon salt and stir with clean rubber spatula to combine.

3　Add beef, Parmesan, garlic powder, oregano, and remaining ½ teaspoon salt to bowl with panko mixture and mix together with your hands.

4　Divide beef mixture into 12 portions (about 3 tablespoons each) and place on plate. Use your slightly wet hands to roll each portion into ball.

5　Add meatballs to sauce in pot.

6　Bring sauce to simmer over medium heat. Cover and cook until meatballs are cooked through, 15 to 18 minutes, stirring halfway through cooking. Serve.

Notes Use this space to write what you liked (or didn't like) about this recipe or draw a picture of what you made!

Food for Thought

While your meatballs cook, take a bite out of these meaty math problems.

If your family starts dinner with 12 meatballs and each person eats 2 meatballs for dinner, how many meatballs are left?

If you are serving meatballs to 6 people and each person wants 3 meatballs, how many meatballs do you need to make?

Your recipe makes 12 meatballs. If you want to save half of the meatballs for tomorrow, how many meatballs should you eat today?

SEE PAGE 130 FOR ANSWERS

Bean and Cheese Quesadillas

SERVES 2

TOTAL TIME 25 minutes

Eat these quesadillas plain or serve them with salsa, sour cream, and/or guacamole.

Prepare Ingredients

⅓ cup canned black beans

2 teaspoons plus 1 teaspoon extra-virgin olive oil, measured separately

2 (8-inch) flour tortillas

⅔ cup shredded Monterey Jack cheese

Gather Cooking Equipment

Colander

Medium bowl

Fork

Rimmed baking sheet

Pastry brush

Oven mitts

Cooling rack

Spatula

Cutting board

Chef's knife

Start Cooking!

1 Adjust oven rack to middle position and heat oven to 450 degrees. Set colander in sink. Pour beans into colander. Rinse beans with cold water and shake colander to drain well. Add beans and 2 teaspoons oil to bowl. Use fork to mash beans to chunky paste.

2 Place tortillas on rimmed baking sheet. Use pastry brush to paint tortillas with remaining 1 teaspoon oil. Flip tortillas over so oiled side is on baking sheet.

3 Use fork to spread half of bean mixture over half of each tortilla. Sprinkle cheese over bean mixture. Fold tortillas in half, forming half-moon shape, and press to flatten.

4 Place baking sheet in oven and bake quesadillas until spotty brown, 5 to 7 minutes.

5 Use oven mitts to remove baking sheet from oven (ask an adult for help). Place baking sheet on cooling rack and let quesadillas cool on baking sheet for 5 minutes.

6 Use spatula to transfer quesadillas to cutting board. Cut into wedges. Serve.

Notes Use this space to write what you liked (or didn't like) about this recipe or draw a picture of what you made!

Food for Thought

While quesadilla might be a tough word to rhyme, lots of other words in this recipe are prime for a rhyme. How many words can you think of that rhyme with the words below? We added some examples for inspiration.

MASH	crash

BEAN	green

CHEESE	please

BAKE	snake

SEE PAGE 130 FOR HINTS

Buttermilk Drop Biscuits

MAKES 10 biscuits

TOTAL TIME 45 minutes, plus cooling time

Prepare Ingredients

2 cups (10 ounces) all-purpose flour

2 teaspoons baking powder

½ teaspoon baking soda

1 teaspoon sugar

¾ teaspoon salt

1 cup buttermilk

8 tablespoons unsalted butter, melted

Vegetable oil spray

Gather Cooking Equipment

Rimmed baking sheet

Parchment paper

Large bowl

Whisk

Liquid measuring cup

Fork

Rubber spatula

¼-cup dry measuring cup

Oven mitts

Cooling rack

Start Cooking!

1 Adjust oven rack to middle position and heat oven to 450 degrees. Line rimmed baking sheet with parchment paper.

2 In large bowl, whisk flour, baking powder, baking soda, sugar, and salt until combined. In liquid measuring cup, use fork to stir buttermilk and melted butter until butter forms small clumps.

3 Add buttermilk mixture to bowl with flour mixture. Use rubber spatula to stir until just combined.

4 Spray inside of ¼-cup dry measuring cup with vegetable oil spray. Use greased measuring cup to scoop batter. Use rubber spatula to scrape off extra batter. Drop scoops onto baking sheet to make 10 biscuits (leave space between biscuits and respray measuring cup as needed).

5 Place baking sheet in oven and bake biscuits until tops are golden brown 12 to 14 minutes. Use oven mitts to remove baking sheet from oven (ask an adult for help). Place baking sheet on cooling rack. Let biscuits cool on baking sheet for 10 minutes. Serve warm.

Food for Thought

These light, fluffy biscuits get their name because you **drop** the batter onto the baking sheet. In this recipe, you used a ¼-cup dry measuring cup to scoop and drop 10 biscuits onto the rimmed baking sheet. Can you work backwards and figure out how many cups of biscuit batter you started with? Remember, there are four ¼ cups in 1 cup.

Notes Use this space to write what you liked (or didn't like) about this recipe or draw a picture of what you made!

SEE PAGE 130 FOR ANSWER

Giant Chocolate Chip Cookie

SERVES 12
TOTAL TIME 45 minutes, plus cooling time

If you don't have a springform pan, you can use a 9-inch round cake pan instead (you'll flip the cookie out of the pan just like a cake).

Prepare Ingredients

Vegetable oil spray

1 cup (5 ounces) all-purpose flour

¼ teaspoon baking soda

¼ teaspoon salt

8 tablespoons unsalted butter, melted

½ cup packed (3½ ounces) dark brown sugar

¼ cup (1¾ ounces) sugar

1 large egg

1 teaspoon vanilla extract

½ cup (3 ounces) chocolate chips

Gather Cooking Equipment

9-inch springform pan

2 bowls (1 large, 1 medium)

Whisk

Rubber spatula

Oven mitts

Cooling rack

Butter knife

Icing spatula or wide metal spatula

Cutting board

Chef's knife

Start Cooking!

1 Adjust oven rack to upper-middle position and heat oven to 375 degrees. Spray inside bottom and sides of 9-inch springform pan with vegetable oil spray.

2 In medium bowl, whisk together flour, baking soda, and salt.

3 In large bowl, whisk melted butter, brown sugar, and sugar until well combined. Add egg and vanilla and whisk until smooth.

Notes Use this space to write what you liked (or didn't like) about this recipe or draw a picture of what you made!

4 Add flour mixture to large bowl with butter mixture and use rubber spatula to stir until just combined and no dry flour is visible, about 1 minute. Add chocolate chips and stir until evenly distributed.

5 Use rubber spatula to scrape cookie dough into greased springform pan and spread dough into even layer covering bottom of pan.

6 Place springform pan in oven and bake until cookie is golden brown and edges are set, 18 to 22 minutes.

7 Use oven mitts to remove springform pan from oven (ask an adult for help). Place springform pan on cooling rack and let cookie cool in pan for 30 minutes.

8 Run butter knife around inside edge of springform pan to loosen edges of cookie from pan. Unlock and remove side of pan. Use icing spatula or wide metal spatula to loosen bottom of cookie from pan and transfer cookie to cutting board. Cut cookie into wedges and serve warm.

Food for Thought

Your Giant Chocolate Chip Cookie makes enough for 12 servings. How will you cut the circle into 12 equal cookie wedges?

 First, cut your cookie in half. How many equal pieces do you have?

 Then, cut your cookie in fourths. How many equal pieces do you have now?

 How will you turn ¼ of a cookie into ½₂ of a cookie? (Cut each ¼ into 3 equal pieces.)

After-School Peanut Butter Cookies

MAKES 12 cookies
TOTAL TIME 30 minutes, plus cooling time

Be sure to use creamy peanut butter in this recipe—chunky peanut butter will result in cookies that won't hold together as well.

Prepare Ingredients

½ cup (3½ ounces) sugar

1 large egg

½ cup creamy peanut butter

¼ cup M&M'S or Reese's Pieces, or 12 Hershey's Kisses

Gather Cooking Equipment

Rimmed baking sheet	1-tablespoon measuring spoon
Parchment paper	Small spoon
Large bowl	Oven mitts
Whisk	Cooling rack
Rubber spatula	Spatula

Start Cooking!

1 Adjust oven rack to middle position and heat oven to 350 degrees. Line rimmed baking sheet with parchment paper.

2 In large bowl, whisk sugar and egg until smooth. Let mixture sit until sugar dissolves, about 5 minutes.

3 Add peanut butter to bowl and use rubber spatula to stir until smooth.

4 Use 1-tablespoon measuring spoon to drop 12 scoops of dough onto baking sheet, leaving space between scoops. (Dough is sticky so use small spoon to scrape from measuring spoon onto baking sheet). Gently press candies into tops of cookies.

5 Place baking sheet in oven. Bake cookies until edges are golden and tops are set, 10 to 12 minutes.

6 Use oven mitts to remove baking sheet from oven (ask an adult for help). Place baking sheet on cooling rack and let cookies cool on baking sheet for 10 minutes.

7 Use spatula to transfer cookies directly to cooling rack and let cool for 5 minutes before serving.

Notes Use this space to write what you liked (or didn't like) about this recipe or draw a picture of what you made!

Food for Thought

If you're using M&M's or Reese's Pieces in these cookies, you might be wondering how many candies to press into each cookie so that they'll all have the same number? Math to the rescue! To find out how many candies to press into each cookie:

- First, count how many candies are in ¼ cup.

- Then, divide that number by 12 (the number of cookies you'll make).

Don't worry if the answer isn't an even number—it's OK if some cookies have more (or fewer) candies than others!

S'mores Rice Cereal Treats

MAKES 16 bars

TOTAL TIME 25 minutes, plus 1 hour setting time

Be sure to use large marshmallows in this recipe as mini ones won't melt as well.

Prepare Ingredients

Vegetable oil spray

1 (10-ounce) package large marshmallows

4 tablespoons unsalted butter

1 teaspoon vanilla extract

⅛ teaspoon salt

5 cups (5 ounces) crisped rice cereal

½ cup (3 ounces) chocolate chips

3 whole graham crackers, broken into small pieces

Gather Cooking Equipment

8-inch square metal baking pan

Rubber spatula

Large microwave-safe bowl

Oven mitts

Butter knife

Cutting board

Chef's knife

Start Cooking!

1 Spray inside bottom and sides of 8-inch square metal baking pan well with vegetable oil spray. Spray rubber spatula with vegetable oil spray.

2 In large microwave-safe bowl, combine marshmallows, butter, vanilla, and salt. Heat in microwave until marshmallows are puffed, about 2 minutes. Use oven mitts to remove bowl from microwave. Use greased rubber spatula to stir until smooth.

3 Add cereal, chocolate chips, and graham cracker pieces to bowl. Stir until well combined. Scrape cereal mixture onto greased baking pan.

4 Lightly wet your hands and press cereal mixture into flat, even layer. Let sit at room temperature for 1 hour to set. Run butter knife around edge of cereal treats to loosen from baking pan. Flip cereal treats out of pan and transfer to cutting board. Cut into squares and serve.

Notes Use this space to write what you liked (or didn't like) about this recipe or draw a picture of what you made!

Food for Thought

Rice Krispies, a type of crisped rice cereal made by the Kellogg's company, is one of the most popular types of cereal on supermarket shelves—and a key ingredient in this recipe. Rice Krispies cereal was invented in 1927, but according to legend, Rice Krispies Treats weren't invented until the 1930s when Mildred Day, a Kellogg's recipe tester, combined marshmallows and the crisped rice cereal. Originally called "marshmallow squares," Kellogg's printed the recipe for the new treat on its Rice Krispies cereal box for the first time in 1941. Families have been making and eating them ever since!

Imagine you are an inventor like Mildred Day. Can you imagine a new treat that uses breakfast cereal as an ingredient? Draw a picture of your idea in the box at right and think of a name for it.

My treats are called:

What type of cereal would you use in your recipe?

What other ingredients would your treat have?

If you're feeling adventurous, try to make a batch of your new treat and do a taste test with your family!

Fudgy Chocolate Mug Cakes

SERVES 2
TOTAL TIME 30 minutes

These cakes "bake" for just a few minutes in the microwave!

Prepare Ingredients

¼ cup (1¼ ounces) all-purpose flour

½ teaspoon baking powder

4 tablespoons unsalted butter, cut into 4 pieces

3 tablespoons chocolate chips

2 large eggs

¼ cup (1¾ ounces) sugar

2 tablespoons cocoa powder

1 teaspoon vanilla extract

⅛ teaspoon salt

Gather Cooking Equipment

2 bowls (1 small, 1 medium microwave-safe)

Whisk

Spoon

2 coffee mugs (at least 11 ounces each)

Oven mitts

Start Cooking!

1 In small bowl, whisk together flour and baking powder.

2 In medium microwave-safe bowl, combine butter and chocolate chips. Heat in microwave at 50 percent power for 1 minute. Open microwave and stir mixture with spoon. Continue to heat in microwave at 50 percent power until melted, about 1 minute. Remove bowl from microwave.

3 Add eggs, sugar, cocoa, vanilla, and salt to medium microwave-safe bowl with chocolate mixture and whisk until smooth.

4 Add flour mixture and whisk until smooth. Use spoon to divide batter evenly between 2 coffee mugs.

5 Place mugs on opposite sides of microwave turntable. Cook in microwave at 50 percent power for 1 minute. Open microwave and use spoon to stir batter in each mug, making sure to reach bottom of mug.

6 Cook in microwave at 50 percent power for 1 minute (batter will rise to just below rim of mug and cake should look slightly wet around edges—if top still looks very wet, cook in microwave at 50 percent power for another 15 to 30 seconds).

7 Use oven mitts to remove mugs from microwave and let cool for 5 minutes. Serve warm.

Notes Use this space to write what you liked (or didn't like) about this recipe or draw a picture of what you made!

Food for Thought

You've probably popped popcorn or heated up food (and now baked a cake!) in the microwave. But have you ever wondered how microwave ovens work?

Microwave ovens generate invisible electromagnetic waves (called . . . microwaves!). Those microwaves make water molecules heat up. And there's a *lot* of water in food. Wherever the microwaves strike the food, the water molecules heat up. That heat spreads from one part of the food to other parts—usually from the outside to the inside—heating up more of the food over time. You can see this in action as you "bake" your mug cakes in the microwave.

1 Observe your mug cake before you put it in the microwave. Is it liquid or solid?

2 Observe your mug cake when you stir the batter in step 5. Is it liquid? Solid? Or a combination? Does it look different before and after you stir?

3 Observe your mug cake one more time, right before you eat it. Is it liquid? Solid? Or a combination?

The sandwich was invented in England almost 300 years ago, when the fourth Earl of Sandwich, a member of the British nobility, was too busy to sit down to a meal. Instead, he asked to be served slices of cold beef between two pieces of bread . . . and the rest is sandwich history. Today, you hold the reigns of sandwich power: Design YOUR dream sandwich. One that you'd be excited to eat for lunch. (Or dinner, or breakfast—it's always a good time for sandwiches!) The only rule? It's got to have bread and fillings. Otherwise, the sky's the limit.

To ignite your imagination, think about the different parts of a sandwich:

The Bread

What will you use for the outside of your sandwich? There are so many options: pillowy sandwich bread, chewy sourdough, a pita pocket, a lavash wrap, even a tortilla! Will you toast your bread or leave it plain? Will your sandwich be closed- or open-face?

The Filling

What will be your main filling? Will you go traditional with sliced turkey, ham, or cheese? Add leftovers, such as grilled chicken, meatballs, or falafel? Or will you use a creamy spread, such as hummus or peanut butter? You could even use scrambled eggs to make a breakfast sandwich!

The Extras

What will you use to add more flavors and textures to your sandwich? Smooth mayonnaise or sliced avocado? Tangy barbecue sauce? Spicy mustard? Some crunch from shredded carrots, cooked bacon, or a few potato chips? A bit of sweetness from jam or honey?

My Dream Sandwich

Draw a picture in the space below. Label the parts of your sandwich. Give your sandwich a name, too!

Make It Your Way Challenge: Get Salty

Salt is an amazing ingredient. Not only does salt have its own taste (put a few grains on your tongue—what does it taste like?), it also amps up the flavor of just about any food it's added to.

Today your task is to discover what foods taste even better with a sprinkle of salt. Explore your pantry, refrigerator, freezer, or garden and gather foods that you think might taste better with some salt. Look for some savory foods and some sweet ones. Take a bite or sip of each food without salt. Then, taste again after you add some salt. How does the flavor change? Don't be afraid to try something totally wacky—you never know what will taste better with a few flakes of salt!

Salt Sources

Try sprinkling coarse sea salt (or even kosher salt) on different foods. Then, take a taste. How does adding salt change the food's flavor? You can even try adding a dash of a salty condiment, such as soy sauce or Worcestershire sauce.

Here are some ideas to spark your salty exploration:

FRUITS Watermelon, honeydew, peaches, grapefruit, mangos, berries

VEGETABLES Tomatoes, potatoes, radishes, broccoli, corn on the cob

GRAINS & BREADS Rice, pasta, buttered toast, oatmeal, popcorn

PROTEINS Eggs, steak, salmon, nuts, nut butter

DAIRY Butter, pudding, yogurt, cheese, ice cream

SWEETS Chocolate bars, cookies, caramel sauce, pies, frosting

BEVERAGES Fruit juice, hot cocoa, smoothies

Foods That Tasted Better with Salt
Draw pictures or keep a list of the foods that you've tried with salt in the space below.

It's fun to experience different textures when you're eating a meal or even a single bite of food: smooth yogurt with crunchy granola, creamy ice cream with gooey hot fudge, tender pancakes with sticky maple syrup . . . and on and on and on!

Can you create a snack or meal that includes at least THREE different textures? You can make something savory (such as a sandwich or salad), or something sweet (like an ice cream sundae). Breakfast, lunch, dinner, snack, dessert—anything goes! See what foods you already have in the pantry or refrigerator, or ask an adult to help you visit the grocery store.

Here are some suggestions to help you brainstorm different texture combinations:

SMOOTH Yogurt, tomato soup, mashed potatoes, avocado

MOIST Strawberries, banana bread, chocolate cake, tomatoes, watermelon, pound cake

STICKY Honey, jam, maple syrup, caramel sauce, peanut butter

CRUNCHY Cereal, apples, fried chicken, nuts, pretzels, granola, celery

DRY Dried herbs, toasted bread, popcorn, saltines

CREAMY Ice cream, Brie cheese, mayonnaise, pudding

CRISPY Cooked bacon, romaine lettuce, potato chips

CHEWY Brownies, beef jerky, gummy candies, al dente pasta, caramel candies

CRUMBLY Shortbread cookies, corn on the cob, biscuits, rice, feta cheese

SOFT Hamburger buns, marshmallows, dinner rolls, muffins, bananas

TENDER Braised meat, mozzarella cheese, cooked beans, pancakes

CHUNKY Vegetable soup, chili, cottage cheese, guacamole, salsa

My Food Texture Creation

Draw a picture in the space below. What textures did your dish feature?

Texture 1

Texture 2

Texture 3

More Textures

Make It Your Way Challenge:
Cheese Snack Plate

Cheese and crackers are a classic snack pairing. They're also a blank canvas that lets your imagination run wild.

Today we challenge you to create your ideal cheese snack plate! It can be small or large, sweet or savory—or both! Put together a plate full of different colors or stick with one hue and make it monochrome (why not!?). Mix and match flavors and textures: creamy, crunchy, salty, gooey, crispy, nutty, sweet . . . see if you can build a different combination for every bite!

To inspire your cheesy brainstorming, think about the three things that most cheese plates have:

The Base

What will you put your cheese on top of? Usually this is something crispy or crunchy, such as crackers, pita chips, or even potato chips. You could also use something sweet, such as slices of fresh fruit or even a waffle or pancake!

The Cheese

You can't have a cheese snack plate without cheese! If you want to include more than one cheese, try using cheeses with different textures, such as a hard cheddar and a soft Brie.

The Extras

Add layers of flavor and texture (and color!) to your snack plate with one or more extras. Will you try something sweet, such as fruit, honey, or jam? Something savory, such as sliced ham or salami? Sour pickles? Crunchy nuts? Fresh herbs? Spicy salsa? Anything goes!

My Cheese Snack Plate

Draw a picture in the space below. Label the different parts.

Sketch Lots of scientists work in labs, but only a few scientists work in recipe labs—draw what you think a recipe lab looks like on this page!

CHAPTER 2 Science Experiments and Activities

= **Activity**   = **Experiment**

The Nose KNOWS

TOTAL TIME 10 minutes

Does what you smell change what you taste? Find out with this supereasy taste test. Jelly Belly jelly beans have very intense flavors and work the best in this experiment.

Materials

1 bag Jelly Belly jelly beans

1 small bowl

1 blindfold per taster (optional)

Get Started!

1 Empty bag of jelly beans into bowl.

2 **Make a prediction:** Do you think a jelly bean's flavor changes if you hold your nose while you eat it? Why or why not?

3 Close your eyes or put on your blindfold—no peeking! With 2 fingers, pinch your nose closed.

Read through the rest of the steps before you close your eyes!

4 Keep pinching your nose. With your other hand, pick up 1 jelly bean. Put it in your mouth. Chew it while you slowly count to 3 in your head. Can you tell what flavor it is? What does it taste like?

5 **Observe your results:** Let go of your nose. Breathe in and out as you chew the jelly bean. Slowly count to 3 in your head again. Swallow the jelly bean. Is the taste different when you let go of your nose? How so? Can you tell what flavor the jelly bean is?

6 Repeat with more jelly beans. If you're doing this experiment with friends, take turns picking out jelly beans for others to taste and guess the flavor (only the picker should be able to see the jelly beans). How often can tasters correctly identify the jelly bean's flavor when they're holding their noses? How about when they let go?

Notes Use this space to write or draw your observations—or simply record your favorite jelly bean flavor!

Fun Fact!
Did you ever notice that when you have a stuffy nose, a lot of foods just taste kind of, well, blah? That's because your stuffy nose prevents some air from moving through your nose, which limits your retronasal olfaction (see below!).

STOP

UNDERSTANDING YOUR RESULTS

Don't read until you've finished the experiment!

Could you tell the flavor of your jelly bean when you were pinching your nose? We did this experiment in the America's Test Kitchen Kids lab and every single person had trouble identifying the jelly bean flavors when they held their noses. "It just tastes sweet, like sugar," said one taster. But as soon as they let go of their noses, all the tasters could immediately tell what flavor jelly bean they were eating. Is this what you observed, too?

So what's going on? Why do jelly beans have ZERO flavor when you hold your nose and then a ton of flavor when you can breathe in and out? First, we need to break down the difference between taste and flavor. They're actually not the same thing. (Surprise!)

We get the taste of a food from the tastebuds in our mouth and on our tongue. They tell you if something is sweet, sour, salty, bitter, or umami (which is a meaty, savory taste). When you

chewed the jelly bean with your nose closed, your tastebuds detected that it was sweet, since jelly beans contain a lot of sugar.

But there's more going on here. When you're chewing, you're also breathing in and out through your nose. When you breathe out, the smell of whatever you're chewing flows from your mouth up into your nose. The smell gets to your nose through a passage at the back of your mouth. This way of smelling is known as retronasal olfaction ("ret-tro-NAY-zal ol-FACK-shun"). Say that five times fast. (You also can detect smells when you breathe in through your nose—this is just called olfaction. Not quite as fun to say.)

When you let go of your nose and chewed the jelly bean, its smell traveled up into your nose. Suddenly, your brain could put together what your nose knew and what your tastebuds tasted, and ta-da! You figured out the flavor of the jelly bean!

The Many Shades of
FLAVOR

 TOTAL TIME 20 minutes

In this activity, **YOU** are the scientist! Your research question? Does a food's color affect what we think of its flavor? To answer this question, you'll have unsuspecting "subjects" (your friends and family) taste two different samples of apple juice—one plain and one that you dyed red with (flavorless) food coloring. Shhh! Don't give it away!

Materials

½ cup apple juice per taster

Red food coloring (liquid, not gel)

2 small, clear drinking glasses per taster

Masking tape or sticky notes

Marker or pen

Liquid measuring cup

Spoon

1 piece of scrap paper per taster

1 pen or pencil per taster

Get Started!

1 Figure out how many subjects you will have for your experiment. (When scientists are conducting research, their "subjects" are the people whose reactions or responses they're studying.) You can tell your subjects that you're looking for their opinions on some samples of juice. **Don't tell them anything else about the experiment at this point!** You don't want to sway their thoughts.

2 In a separate room (or somewhere your subjects can't see you), prepare a set of juice samples for each subject. Use masking tape and marker to label 1 glass as "A" and 1 glass as "B." Add ¼ cup of apple juice to glass A. Add another ¼ cup of apple juice to glass B.

3 Add 5 to 8 drops of red food coloring to all the glasses labeled "A." Use spoon to stir each glass until color is evenly distributed. You want your juice to look bright red—think fruit punch or cranberry juice. (Working with food coloring can stain your hands, so you might want to wear gloves for this part of the experiment.)

4 Set up your experiment on a table or counter. Create a spot for each of your subjects with 1 glass of sample A, 1 glass of sample B, 1 piece of scrap paper, and 1 pen or pencil.

5 Make a prediction: Do you think your subjects will think the two glasses of juice will taste the same or different? Why do you think so?

6 Call in your subjects! Have each of them sit or stand at 1 of the spots you set up. Explain what they need to do; you could say something like this:

- You have 2 samples of juice in front of you, sample A and sample B.

- Take a few sips of each sample and think about their flavors. Do they taste sweet? Sour? Bitter? Does the flavor remind you of anything? Which sample do you like better, A or B?

- You can jot down notes on the scrap paper at your spot. Don't say anything out loud about the samples until everyone is ready! You don't want to influence others' opinions.

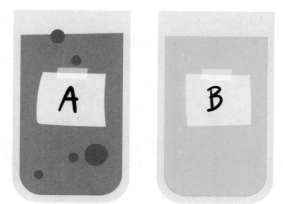

turn the page!

7 Observe your results: Once all subjects have finished tasting and thinking, ask them to tell you what they thought of each sample's flavor. Have subjects vote for which juice they preferred, A or B, by a show of hands.

8 Time for the big reveal! Tell your subjects that you played a (small) trick on them—in the name of science! The juice in samples A and B was the same—both glasses contained apple juice, but sample A was dyed red. Were your subjects surprised?

9 Ask them to taste the 2 juice samples again, this time with their eyes closed. What do they think of the flavor of the samples now? Do they taste the same? Do they still taste different?

Notes Use this space to write or draw your observations from this experiment.

How many of your subjects believed that these were two different juices? When we tried this experiment in the America's Test Kitchen Kids lab, **NONE** of our subjects realized that both glasses contained apple juice. Everyone thought they were two different kinds of juice! Some of our subjects thought the red juice might be strawberry, cherry, or fruit punch flavor. A few did identify the plain (non-dyed) juice as apple juice.

Why was it so easy to trick our subjects into believing they were tasting two different juices, just by changing the color? Scientists have been investigating this question for more than 50 years, and they still don't have all the answers—maybe you'll figure some of them out!

Here's some of what we DO know: As we grow up and taste lots of different foods and drinks, our brains come to associate certain flavors with certain colors. We connect yellow with lemon, green with lime, red with strawberry or cherry, and blue with . . . blue flavor? You get the picture. And those connections are really strong. When we **see** a drink that's red, our brain already starts to think, "That's probably strawberry, or cherry, or cranberry," even before we take a sip. When we taste a food or drink that's the "wrong" color, such as apple juice that's been dyed red, our brains have a hard time ignoring the color and using taste and smell to identify flavor.

An extreme example of how food's color affects what we taste came from a study in which researchers served people a dinner of steak, french fries, and peas. Delicious, right? The only strange thing was that the subjects were eating dinner pretty much in the dark. Then, partway through dinner, the researchers turned up the lights. The subjects saw that the steak had been dyed blue, the french fries dyed green, and the peas dyed red. Let's just say that many of them suddenly felt very sick, even though the food was perfectly fine—and tasted delectable just moments before. Behold the power of color.

Take It Further

Want to do some more experimenting with color and flavor? Try serving subjects vanilla pudding alongside vanilla pudding that you dyed brown (use gel food coloring here)—do your subjects think the brown pudding is chocolate-flavored? Or try dying lemon-lime soda with orange food coloring—do your subjects think it's orange soda? What other foods can you think of to try this with? Use the space below to record what other foods you tried this with—and your results.

What Makes Fizzy Drinks FIZZY?

TOTAL TIME 10 minutes

Have you ever noticed that the bubbles only appear in a fizzy bottle of soda or seltzer AFTER you open the bottle? In this experiment, you'll discover the origins of those bouncing bubbles.

Materials

3 cups (24 ounces) plain seltzer, chilled

2 raisins or dried cranberries

2 tall, clear drinking glasses, both the same size and shape

1 clean marble or ball bearing

Spoon

Get Started!

1 **Make a prediction:** Which do you think will create more bubbles: Dropping a raisin or dropping a marble into a glass of seltzer? Why do you think so?

2 Fill both drinking glasses with cold seltzer until they are about ¾ full (be sure to fill both glasses to the same level).

3 Place glasses side by side on counter. Hold marble about 1 inch above surface of seltzer in 1 glass. Hold raisin about 1 inch above surface of seltzer in second glass (make sure marble and raisin are at same height).

4 **Observe your results:** Let go of marble and raisin at same time, letting them drop into their respective glasses. Observe what happens for 30 seconds.

5 Use spoon to retrieve marble and raisin from the glasses. Repeat steps 3 and 4 with marble and second raisin. This time, observe what happens for at least 5 minutes. How do your results compare with your prediction?

Notes Use this space to write or draw your observations from this experiment.

UNDERSTANDING YOUR RESULTS

Don't read until you've finished the experiment!

The bubbles in seltzer or soda are made of carbon dioxide gas. When seltzer is in a sealed bottle, the gas is dissolved in the liquid—you can't see it. When you open the bottle, some of the dissolved carbon dioxide turns back into a gas and escapes as bubbles. But to get the bubbles really popping, you need help.

Just like Clark Kent needs a phone booth to change into Superman, dissolved carbon dioxide needs a special place to become a bubble, called a nucleation ("new-clee-AY-shun") site. Bubbles form at nucleation sites and rise through the beverage until they pop at the surface. A nucleation site can be anything from a tiny fiber from a towel to the surfaces of the marble and raisin.

The wrinkly raisin has more nucleation sites than the smooth marble. **And more nucleation sites means more bubbles!** But there's only so much carbon dioxide dissolved in the water. Eventually, the bubbles slow down because there's not much carbon dioxide left. The gas is used up more quickly when there are more nucleation sites, as in the glass with the raisin.

SALT ART

TOTAL TIME 25 minutes

Salt doesn't just make foods tastier—it can also help create colorful works of art! The number of bowls you need depends on your type of watercolor paints. For dry pans of paint, you'll need two bowls, one for the salt and one for water. For liquid watercolor paints, you'll need one bowl for salt, one bowl for water, and one bowl for each color paint.

Materials

Pencil

Watercolor paper or card stock

Rimmed baking sheet

White glue

1 cup kosher salt

2 (or more) small bowls

Small paintbrush

Watercolor paints

Water

Get Started!

1 **Decide on your design:** Will you create a picture of something (or someone), or an interesting pattern? Use pencil to sketch or trace an outline of your design on watercolor paper.

2 Place paper inside rimmed baking sheet. Carefully squeeze white glue from bottle over your pencil outline— add glue wherever you want there to be color on your design.

3 Add salt to 1 small bowl. Use your fingers to generously sprinkle salt all over glue (paint won't stick to any spots of glue not covered in salt).

4 Carefully pick up paper and gently shake off excess salt onto baking sheet. Let glue dry for 5 minutes. Ask an adult to help you pour excess salt back into bowl. (Reuse the remaining salt to create another artwork, but do not use it for cooking or eating.)

5 Load paintbrush with paint. Gently touch paintbrush to salt to add color. Don't swipe or move paintbrush— the paint will naturally travel along salt-covered outlines of your design.

6 Continue loading paintbrush with paint and touching paintbrush to salt. If you want to switch colors, be sure to thoroughly rinse paintbrush in water before dipping it in new color of paint.

7 After you've finished adding color to your design, set aside paper where it won't be disturbed. Let dry for at least 2 hours. Then, display your artwork!

Sketch Use this space to practice sketching your picture or design.

Food for Thought

Why does the watercolor paint color the salt, but not the paper below? It's all thanks to the special relationship between salt and water. Salt is hygroscopic ("hi-grow-SKAH-pick"). That means it's REALLY good at absorbing water from its surroundings. Don't believe us? Try dripping some water onto the extra salt left over from making your salt art. The salt should absorb the water almost instantly.

Watercolor paint is made of mostly—you guessed it—water! When you touch the salt with the watercolor paint, the salt, like a sponge, quickly absorbs the paint. There's no paint left over to reach the paper below.

Fill in the Gaps
Here's another way to use salt and watercolor paint to make art! Use your paintbrush to paint a large area on a sheet of watercolor paper, making sure to use plenty of water. While the paint is still wet, sprinkle a little kosher salt onto the paint, and then observe. The salt will create a pretty pattern as it absorbs the water in the paint!

Be a Salt
FARMER

MAKES About 1 tablespoon flaky salt
TOTAL TIME 10 minutes, plus 24–48 hours evaporation time

Humans have been harvesting salt since prehistoric times. Try it yourself by creating a model ocean and harvesting your own chunky, flaky salt! Tap water can contain tiny dissolved minerals that are safe to drink but can give your salt a bitter flavor.

Materials

¼ cup distilled or filtered water

2 tablespoons kosher salt

Liquid measuring cup

Oven mitts

1-teaspoon measuring spoon

Spoon

Coffee filter

8-inch square glass baking dish or pie plate

Hand lens (optional)

> This flaky, chunky salt is great for sprinkling on finished dishes, such as eggs, vegetables, fruits, meats, and more. Check out the Make It Your Way Challenge: Get Salty (page 46) and discover what foods taste better with a sprinkle of salt!

Get Started!

1 Add water to liquid measuring cup. Heat in microwave until water is steaming, 1 to 1½ minutes. Use oven mitts to remove measuring cup from microwave (ask an adult for help).

2 Add 1 teaspoon of salt to hot water. Stir with spoon until salt is completely dissolved and water is clear. Continue adding salt, 1 teaspoon at a time, and stirring until all salt is dissolved into water. If there are undissolved salt crystals after you've added all the salt, strain solution through coffee filter before continuing with step 3.

Notes Use this space to write or draw your observations from this activity—and record what you sprinkled your salt on!

3 Set baking dish in place where it won't be disturbed. (A warm, sunny spot will help speed up evaporation.) Carefully pour saltwater into baking dish—this is your model of the ocean.

4 Leave baking dish undisturbed for 24 to 48 hours, or until all water has evaporated. Use hand lens, if you have one, to observe model ocean a few times as it evaporates. What do you notice?

5 Harvest your salt! Use spoon to gently scrape salt from bottom of baking dish (salt will form large chunks). Salt can be stored in airtight container indefinitely.

Food for Thought

The big square or rectangular salt crystals you harvested actually came from the tiny crystals of kosher salt you started with! When you dissolve salt in hot water and then let the water slowly cool and evaporate, the structure of the salt crystals left behind can change.

When mixed with water, salt crystals dissolve into tiny ions. The hotter the water, the more salt you can dissolve into it. When dissolved salt ions find one another, they lock together (kind of like puzzle pieces) and fall out of the solution. As more salt joins them, the crystal grows bigger and bigger. The slower a salt solution cools, the more time the salt ions have to find one another and grow larger crystals. Since you let your salt solution cool slowly, you were able to form some big salt crystals!

Testing and Tasting
TEXTURE

MAKES About 1 cup salsa
TOTAL TIME 30 minutes

YOU get to be the scientist in this edible experiment! Your research question: Does changing the texture of a food also change its flavor? Recruit a few volunteers (and make some tasty salsa) to help you find out.

Materials

1 (14.5-ounce) can diced tomatoes, opened

2 slices jarred pickled jalapeño

2 teaspoons lime juice, squeezed from ½ lime

1 garlic clove, peeled

¼ teaspoon salt

¼ cup fresh cilantro leaves

Tortilla chips (optional)

Fine-mesh strainer

3 bowls (1 medium, 2 small)

Rubber spatula

Food processor

Masking tape or sticky notes

Marker

1 blindfold per taster

2 spoons per taster

1 glass of water per taster

Get Started!

PART 1: MAKE YOUR SALSA SAMPLES

1 Set fine-mesh strainer over medium bowl. Pour tomatoes into fine-mesh strainer. Use rubber spatula to stir and press on tomatoes to remove liquid. Let tomatoes drain in strainer for 5 minutes. Discard liquid.

2 Place jalapeño, lime juice, garlic, and salt in food processor. Lock lid into place. Hold down pulse button for 1 second, then release. Repeat until ingredients are roughly chopped, about five 1-second pulses. Remove lid and use rubber spatula to scrape down sides of bowl.

3 Add drained tomatoes to mixture in food processor. Lock lid back into place. Hold down pulse button for 1 second, then release. Repeat until evenly chopped, about three 1-second pulses. Remove lid and carefully remove processor blade (ask an adult for help). Add cilantro to processor and use rubber spatula to stir to combine.

4 Transfer half of salsa to 1 small bowl. Use masking tape and marker to label bowl "Sample A." Set aside.

5 Use rubber spatula to scrape down sides of processor bowl. Replace processor blade (ask an adult for help). Lock lid back into place. Turn on processor and process for about 30 seconds. Stop processor, remove lid, and use rubber spatula to scrape down sides of bowl. Lock lid back into place, turn on processor, and process for another 30 seconds, or until salsa is very smooth.

6 Remove lid and carefully remove processor blade (ask an adult for help). Transfer salsa to second small bowl. Use masking tape and marker to label bowl "Sample B." Set aside, making sure both bowls are out of tasters' sight.

7 **Make a prediction:** Do you think the two salsa samples will taste the same or different? Why do you think so?

PART 2: CONDUCT YOUR EXPERIMENT

1 Recruit some tasters. Explain that they are going to taste 2 different salsas. Their job is to think about the flavor and texture of each salsa.

2 Tell tasters to put on their blindfolds. Give each taster a spoonful of Sample A to eat. Tasters should chew slowly, thinking about the sample's flavor and texture, but should keep their thoughts to themselves for now.

3 Give each taster a glass of water and have them take a sip. Then, give each taster a spoonful of Sample B to eat. If tasters would like, give them more spoonfuls of each salsa to taste.

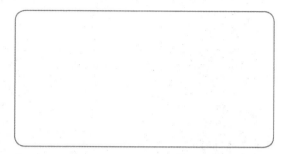

turn the page!

4 Observe your results: Put the 2 salsa samples out of tasters' sight. Have tasters remove their blindfolds. Ask tasters to share what they thought of the texture and flavor of each sample. Could they identify any of the ingredients in either sample?

5 Show tasters the bowls of salsa. Explain that both samples contained the exact same ingredients. The only difference? Their texture. Did tasters think Sample A and Sample B had the same flavor? Could they identify any ingredients in the salsas? (Snack on the rest of your salsa with some tortilla chips!)

Some scientists refer to the way we experience the texture of foods as "mouthfeel." Get it? Texture is the way that foods *feel* inside of our mouth as we eat them.

Notes Use this space to write or draw your observations from this experiment.

STOP ▶ UNDERSTANDING YOUR RESULTS

Don't read until you've finished the experiment!

When we talk about the flavor of food, we're usually referring to a combination of its taste and its smell. **But the way food feels in your mouth as you eat it—its texture—plays a big part in our eating experience.**

Were your tasters able to identify the ingredients in the chunky salsa? How about in the smooth salsa? Did they think the two samples tasted similar or different?

It's often easier to pick out the distinctive flavor and texture of individual ingredients, such as the soft tomato and leafy cilantro, in the chunky salsa. In the smooth salsa, all of the ingredients were processed into tiny pieces, so everything has a similar texture. When you take a bite of smooth salsa, you experience the flavors of lots of ingredients at once, rather than larger pieces of just one or two ingredients.

Take It Further: Snap, Crackle, Science

What happens if you change the iconic texture of a food? Is it as easy to identify what you're eating? See for yourself!

What You'll Need for 4 Tasters

½ cup plus ¼ cup Rice Krispies cereal, measured separately

½ cup plus ¼ cup milk, measured separately

Blender

Dish towel

1-tablespoon measuring spoon

1 blindfold per taster

2 small bowls per taster

1 spoon per taster

Get Started!

1 Place ½ cup Rice Krispies and ½ cup milk in blender. Place lid on top of blender and hold lid firmly in place with folded dish towel. Blend until smooth, about 10 seconds.

2 Prepare 2 samples for each taster: Scoop 2 tablespoons of the blended Rice Krispies–milk mixture into 1 small bowl. In second small bowl, combine 1 tablespoon Rice Krispies and 1 tablespoon milk. (Make sure tasters don't see what you're doing!)

3 Have tasters put on blindfolds. Give tasters blended Rice Krispies–milk mixture and a spoon. As they eat, ask tasters to guess what they are eating— but keep their ideas to themselves for now! Repeat with samples of whole Rice Krispies and milk.

4 Have tasters remove their blindfolds. Ask what they thought about each sample—could they identify what they were eating? Then, tell tasters exactly what they were eating!

Notes Use this space to write or draw your observations from this experiment.

Design Challenge:
PACK IT UP

 TOTAL TIME 25 minutes

Your challenge? Design a package that will protect a single potato chip or cracker from breaking during a fall.

Materials

2–3 Pringles potato crisps, saltines, water crackers, or other thin, fragile chips or crackers

You can use the materials on this list to create your design, or any other supplies around your house!

Cotton balls • Tissue paper • Aluminum foil • Craft sticks • Scrap paper • Tape • Cardboard • Fabric scraps • Brown paper lunch bags • Empty egg carton • Ruler or tape measure • Scissors

Get Started!

1 Your challenge is to design a package for a single potato chip or cracker. Your chip package must:

- Protect the chip from breaking if your package falls onto the floor
- Include a way to put the chip into the package and take it out again, such as a flap, a door, or a latch
- Be smaller than 6 inches in all directions

2 **Gather information:** Look at food packages in your pantry, refrigerator, and freezer, such as egg cartons, cereal boxes, and juice boxes. Which ones protect something fragile inside? How do they do it?

3 **Brainstorm your design:** What materials will you use? Think about what properties might help protect your chip. Do you want to use something flexible? Soft? Thin? Thick? Think about different ways you can use a material. For example, you can roll, fold, or crumple paper.

Sketch It Out Use this space to draw ideas for your design.

4 Build your design: Once you have come up with an idea and decided what materials you will use, it's time to build your design. Keep in mind:

- How will you get your chip into and out of your design?

- Make sure the chip will fit inside your design. (Hint: Use a ruler!)

5 Test your design: Use a ruler to check that your package isn't bigger than 6 inches in any direction. If it is, tweak your design to make it smaller. Use a ruler to measure 4 feet above a hard surface, such as a wood or tile floor. Hold your package at the 4-foot mark and drop it onto the ground. Repeat this 2 more times.

6 Observe your results: Open your package and remove your chip. How easy was it to open your package

Food for Thought

The next time you go to the grocery store, take a closer look at all the different types of food packages. What do you notice? Can you find packages that keep food fresh? How about packages that help you dispense just the right amount of an ingredient? Packages designed to help you eat out of them? What else do you see?

and remove your chip? Is it still in one piece? (Don't worry if your chip broke! When engineers design new technologies, their projects almost never work the first time! They think about what worked—and what didn't work—and then they try again.)

7 Redesign your chip package to make it even better and test it again. What will you change?

Notes Use this space to draw a picture of your final design. Label the parts.

Texture BINGO!

How many different food textures can you find? Play this game with a family member or a friend the next time you're eating together at home. You can also play on your own when you're enjoying breakfast, lunch, a snack, or even dessert!

Materials

1 bingo board per person

9 bingo chips per person (You can use small crackers, pretzels, candies, coins, or buttons as your "chips.")

How to Play

As you're eating, think about the different textures of your food. If you notice a texture that's on one of your bingo-board squares, place a chip on that square. The first player to find three textures in a row—horizontally, vertically, or diagonally—wins!

dry	sticky	crispy
creamy	free space!	thick
crunchy	crumbly	hard

FOOD TEXTURE GLOSSARY

CHUNKY Has pieces of different sizes
CREAMY Thick and rich
CRISPY Firm, dry, and delicate
CRUMBLY Falls apart easily when you bite into it
CRUNCHY Firm; sounds loud when you chew it
DRY Lacks water; feels sandy when you chew it
HARD Solid; requires effort to bite into
SMOOTH Has an even texture without lumps
STICKY Sticks to your teeth when you chew it
THICK Pours slowly, like honey

smooth	crunchy	sticky
chunky	free space!	crispy
hard	smooth	dry

Tasting BLIND

TOTAL TIME 10 minutes

Does what our food looks like affect its flavor? Find out by taking away your sense of sight as you taste two samples of cheese with one big difference—their color. Can you taste a difference if you can't see what you're eating? Make sure your cheeses are either both mild or both sharp cheddar. (Yellow cheddar is actually orange!)

Materials

2 slices white cheddar cheese per taster

2 slices yellow cheddar cheese per taster

1 blindfold per taster

1 small plate per taster

Get Started!

1 **Make a prediction:** Do you think white and yellow cheddar cheese will taste the same or different? Why do you think so?

2 Choose 1 person to give out the cheese samples (this is a good job for an adult). Everyone else will be tasters. Put a small plate in front of each taster and have tasters put on their blindfolds. Tell tasters that they are going to eat 2 pieces of cheddar cheese: 1 piece is white cheddar and 1 is yellow cheddar. Can they tell which is which, if they can't see the cheeses?

3 Once blindfolds are on, place 2 slices **white** cheddar cheese on **left** side of each small plate. Place 2 slices **yellow** cheddar cheese on **right** side of each small plate.

4 Tell tasters to pick up 1 slice of each cheese in each hand and taste it. Which do they think is the white cheddar? The yellow cheddar? Tell tasters to keep their opinions to themselves for now.

5 Observe your results: Once everyone has finished tasting, ask tasters to hold up the remaining slice of cheese that they think is the **white** cheddar. Then, ask tasters to hold up the remaining slice of cheese that they think is the **yellow** cheddar.

6 Have tasters remove their blindfolds and see if they were correct. Then, have tasters taste the remaining slices of cheese without their blindfolds on. What do they notice about the cheeses' flavors now that they can see their colors?

Notes Use this space to keep track of your results: How many tasters correctly identified the white and yellow cheddars?

STOP UNDERSTANDING YOUR RESULTS

Don't read until you've finished the experiment!

Folks in the town Cheddar, England, have been making cheddar cheese for more than 900 years. In the beginning, cheddar cheese was naturally yellow-orange because the cows' milk it's made from also had a yellow-orange hue, thanks to a pigment in the flavorful grass the cows ate during the warmer months. In the cooler seasons, the cow's milk (and the cheese) was white or beige. Cheesemakers eventually realized they could conceal these differences in color by dyeing the white milk bright orange using something called annatto extract. Made from annatto seeds, the dye is completely natural—and tasteless. So, in theory, there shouldn't be any flavor difference between the two colors of cheddar, right?

Many tasters **DO** detect a difference between white and yellow cheddar—though they're usually not sure which color is which when blindfolded. If annatto is flavorless, why can many tasters detect a difference in flavor between the two cheeses?

Today, some manufacturers make their white and yellow cheddars differently. They might use milk from cows that live in different areas and eat different food, which can give their milk different flavors. One type of cheddar might contain more fat or moisture, which can change the cheese's flavor, too.

Do you prefer white or yellow cheddar? The answer likely depends on where you live. White cheddar is more popular along the East Coast of the United States, particularly in the Northeast. The rest of the United States is definitely on team yellow cheddar.

The Gooey Science of MELTING CHEESE

TOTAL TIME 30 minutes

Some cheese melts into gooey deliciousness, while others turn greasy, grainy, or refuse to melt at all. Find out why in this (edible!) experiment. Don't use fresh mozzarella, mild cheddar cheese, or finely grated Parmesan cheese. You can swap the flour tortilla for corn tortillas or even small slices of bread.

Materials

1 (10- to 12-inch) flour tortilla

2 tablespoons shredded mozzarella cheese

2 tablespoons shredded sharp or extra-sharp cheddar cheese

2 tablespoons shredded Parmesan cheese

Cutting board

Chef's knife

Rimmed baking sheet

Masking tape

Marker

Oven mitts

Cooling rack

Get Started!

1 Adjust oven rack to middle position and heat oven to 200 degrees.

2 Use chef's knife to cut tortilla into 3 equal wedges.

3 Arrange tortilla wedges on rimmed baking sheet. Sprinkle mozzarella in even layer on **left** tortilla wedge. Sprinkle cheddar in even layer on **center** tortilla wedge. Sprinkle Parmesan in even layer on **right** tortilla wedge.

4 Use masking tape and marker to label baking sheet "Mozzarella" by left tortilla wedge, "Cheddar" by center tortilla wedge, and "Parmesan" by right tortilla wedge.

5 Make a prediction: Do you think these 3 cheeses will melt the same way? Why do you think so?

6 Place baking sheet in oven and bake for 10 minutes.

7 Use oven mitts to remove baking sheet from oven (ask an adult for help) and place it on cooling rack.

8 Observe your results: Do the melted cheeses look the same? In what ways do they look different? Which would you choose for your grilled cheese sandwich or pizza?

9 Eat your experiment: Snack on any (or all) of your cheesy creations. What do you notice about their flavor? Their texture?

Notes Use this space to write or draw your observations from this experiment.

STOP   *UNDERSTANDING YOUR RESULTS*

Don't read until you've finished the experiment!

Why does mozzarella melt into gooey perfection while Parmesan turns into a greasy mess in the oven? A lot of it has to do with the cheese's age.

Cheese is made of a network of **proteins**, like lots of tiny cages, surrounding bits of **fat** and **water**. When cheese heats up, the fat turns from solid to liquid. Then its proteins loosen up, which makes the cheese "flow" like a thick liquid.

Aged cheeses contain less water than younger cheeses. As cheese ages, it loses water through evaporation (this also concentrates the cheese's flavor). Cheeses with less water don't melt well because their proteins cling together more tightly, making it harder for them to "flow" while also squeezing out droplets of fat.

Parmesan is the oldest of our three cheeses and it barely melts at all. Sharp cheddar is our middle-aged cheese. It melts, but it also leaks some greasy melted fat. Young cheeses—like Monterey Jack, mild cheddar, and mozzarella, which isn't aged at all—are the best choices if you're looking for smooth melted cheese.

The Science of
STRETCHY CHEESE

MAKES 2 grilled cheese sandwiches
TOTAL TIME 25 minutes

Some cheeses stretch. Others don't. Stretch your mind as you test cheese stretchability in this edible experiment! Don't use low-fat or preshredded cheese here. You can swap Monterey Jack, Swiss, or even mild or sharp cheddar for the extra-sharp cheddar.

Materials

4 slices hearty white or wheat sandwich bread

½ cup shredded extra-sharp cheddar cheese

½ cup shredded mozzarella cheese

2 tablespoons unsalted butter

Cutting board

12-inch nonstick skillet

Spatula

Ruler

Get Started!

1 Place bread slices on cutting board. Sprinkle cheddar evenly over 1 slice of bread. Sprinkle mozzarella evenly over second slice of bread. Place 1 bread slice on top of each sandwich and press down gently.

2 In 12-inch nonstick skillet, melt butter over medium-low heat, swirling to evenly coat skillet, about 1 minute.

3 Place sandwiches in skillet and press down on them lightly with spatula. Cook sandwiches until first side is golden brown, 3 to 5 minutes.

4 Use spatula to flip sandwiches and press lightly again. Cook until second side is golden brown and cheese is melted, about 2 minutes.

5 Turn off heat. Use spatula to transfer sandwiches back to cutting board. Let cool for 2 minutes.

6 **Make a prediction:** Which cheese do you think will stretch more when you pull apart your sandwiches: cheddar or mozzarella?

7 Observe your results: Use your hands to gently break cheddar sandwich in half. Hold left half of sandwich in your left hand without moving. Use your right hand to gently pull other half of sandwich to the right. Stop pulling once cheese breaks and is no longer connecting 2 halves of sandwich. How far did the cheese stretch before it broke? Use ruler to measure the length of your cheese pull.

> **Cheddar Cheese Pull**

8 Repeat test with mozzarella sandwich. How far did the cheese stretch before it broke? Use ruler to measure the length of your cheese pull.

> **Mozzarella Cheese Pull**

9 Eat your experiment! Share your grilled cheese sandwiches with a friend or family member while you read about why some cheeses stretch so much more than others.

 **Notes** Use this space to write or draw your observations from this experiment.

 STOP *UNDERSTANDING YOUR RESULTS*
Don't read until you've finished the experiment!

Did your mozzarella cheese stretch much farther than the cheddar cheese?

Why is mozzarella cheese a stretchy superstar? It has a lot to do with the way it's made. Adding acid or enzymes to milk starts the cheese-making process. It causes the milk to separate into solid curds and liquid whey. Those curds get smooshed together into solid cheese.

To make mozzarella, the curds are stretched and pulled over and over again.

During that stretching, proteins in the cheese make their way into very straight lines. When mozzarella is heated, those straight lines of protein loosen up and you can pull the cheese into long strings.

Many other cheeses, such as cheddar, aren't stretched after their curds are pressed together, so their proteins don't form straight lines. When those cheeses melt, their proteins flow in lots of different directions, so the cheese doesn't stretch as much as mozzarella does.

Amazing
EMULSIONS

TOTAL TIME 25 minutes, plus 1 hour observation time

Oil and water don't normally mix. But look at salad dressing: in many of them, oil and vinegar (which is mostly made of water) come together to form a smooth, totally mixed combination—at least for a little while. What's the secret? In this experiment, you'll mix oil and vinegar on their own, with a bit of mustard, and with some mayonnaise. Mustard and mayonnaise are ingredients often found in salad dressings—could they help oil and water play nicely?

Materials

1 cup plus 2 tablespoons extra-virgin olive oil

6 tablespoons red wine vinegar

1 teaspoon Dijon mustard

1 teaspoon mayonnaise

Salt and pepper

Masking tape or sticky notes

Marker or pen

3 (6- to 8-ounce) clear jars with lids

1-tablespoon measuring spoon

Get Started!

1 Use tape and marker to label 1 jar as "Control," second jar as "Mustard," and third jar as "Mayonnaise."

2 Add 6 tablespoons oil and 2 tablespoons vinegar to each jar. Screw lid on jar labeled "Control." Set jar aside.

3 Add mustard to jar labeled "Mustard." Screw lid on tightly. Set jar aside.

4 Add mayonnaise to jar labeled "Mayonnaise" and screw lid on tightly.

5 Hold 1 jar in each hand. Vigorously shake jars for 30 seconds. Set jars aside. Repeat with remaining jar.

6 Make a prediction: In which jar do you predict the oil and vinegar will stay mixed the longest: the control jar, the mustard jar, or the mayonnaise jar? Why do you think so?

7 Observe your results: What do the jars look like right after you finish shaking them? Check on your jars every 15 minutes, until 1 hour has passed. What do you notice? Which jar kept the oil and vinegar mixed the longest? The shortest?

Eat Your Science!

Turn your emulsions into a vinaigrette salad dressing by following these steps.

MAKE DRESSING!

1 Add contents of 1 or more jars into large airtight container with lid.

2 For each jar you combined, add ¼ teaspoon salt and ⅛ teaspoon pepper to container.

3 Cover container and shake to combine ingredients.

4 Dressing will keep in airtight container in the refrigerator for up to 1 week. Shake well before using.

 STOP

UNDERSTANDING YOUR RESULTS

Don't read until you've finished the experiment!

Here in the America's Test Kitchen Kids lab, we found that the jar with mayonnaise stayed mixed the longest, with the mustard jar a close second. The jar with just oil and vinegar separated into layers after less than 15 minutes.

When you shake or whisk oil and vinegar, the two liquids form what's called an emulsion ("ih-MUHL-shun"). **Emulsion** is a science word for a combination of two liquids that don't usually mix, such as oil and water. But this emulsion won't last long—the oil and vinegar retreat into two separate layers after just a few minutes.

To get oil and water to STAY mixed, you need some help from an **emulsifier**.

Emulsifiers are special molecules that bridge the gap between two liquids that don't want to get along, like oil and water. One end of an emulsifier molecule is attracted to water. The other end is attracted to oil (imagine the emulsifier is holding hands with oil on one side and water on the other). Mustard and mayonnaise both contain emulsifiers. A vinaigrette made with an emulsifier will stay combined for much longer than one made with just oil and vinegar.

So which should you use when making a vinaigrette, mustard or mayonnaise? Pick the flavor you like best! Since you add dressing to your salad soon after you mix it, either mustard or mayo works just fine.

Taste Test the RAINBOW

TOTAL TIME 15 minutes

Do different colors of the same vegetable taste different? Round up some family and friends and find out in this colorful taste test! (Not a fan of peppers? Not a problem! Check out Even More Science at right for other veggies you can use instead.)

Materials

1 green bell pepper, stemmed, seeded, and cut into ½-inch strips

1 red bell pepper, stemmed, seeded, and cut into ½-inch strips

1 plate per taster

1 glass of water per taster

1 blindfold per taster

Get Started!

1 **Make a prediction:** Do you think green and red bell peppers taste the same or different? Why do you think so?

2 Choose 1 person to give out the peppers (this is a good job for an adult). Everyone else will be tasters. Give each taster a plate, a glass of water, and a blindfold. Tell tasters they are going to eat 2 pieces of bell pepper. Their job is to observe whether they taste the same or different.

3 Tasters should put on their blindfolds. Place 2 strips of **green** bell pepper on the **left** side of each plate. Place 2 strips of **red** bell pepper on the **right** side of each plate.

4 Blindfolded tasters should pick up 1 strip of pepper at a time and taste it, taking small bites and chewing slowly—but they should keep their opinions about flavors to themselves for now! They can also take sips of water between bites to give their tastebuds a break.

5 Observe your results:
Once everyone has finished tasting both colors of pepper, ask tasters:

- Did you think the 2 peppers tasted the same or different? How so?

6 Have tasters remove their blindfolds. Tell tasters that they tasted two different colors of pepper: green and red. Are they surprised? Have the tasters taste each pepper again, without blindfolds. Do they detect a flavor difference now?

Notes Use this space to write or draw your observations from this experiment.

Even More Science Try this taste test with other vegetables that come in different colors.

- Orange carrots and purple, red, or white carrots
- Red cherry tomatoes and yellow cherry tomatoes
- Red potatoes and purple potatoes (Make sure to cook them first!)

STOP *UNDERSTANDING YOUR RESULTS*
Don't read until you've finished the experiment!

You might want to sit down for this: **Red bell peppers are actually just grown-up green bell peppers.** All peppers start out green. Then, as they ripen on the pepper plant, bell peppers change from green to either yellow or orange, and then, finally, most of them change to red. Green bell peppers are simply harvested before they are fully ripe.

Now let's talk flavor: Green and red bell peppers taste similar, but you might have noticed some flavor differences between them. When we tasted the peppers in the

America's Test Kitchen Kids lab, tasters said the red bell peppers tasted sweeter and fruitier than green bell peppers. The flavor of green bell peppers is often described as "grassy." These observations make sense: As peppers ripen, they create different flavor compounds, which make ripe red peppers taste a bit different from unripe green ones.

Ready for another shock? Peppers are technically fruits, not vegetables, because they contain the seeds of the pepper plant. We call them vegetables because we eat them in savory dishes.

Regrow Your VEGETABLES

TOTAL TIME 5 minutes, plus about 1 week growing time

Lots of recipes use scallions—tacos, stir-fries, lettuce wraps, and more. Next time you're cooking, don't toss your scallion scraps. Instead, use them to grow MORE scallions in just a week! For this activity, try to use scallions with roots that are ½ inch or longer—they will grow fastest.

Materials

Scallions

Water

Chef's knife

Cutting board

Tall drinking glass or jar

Get Started!

1 Use chef's knife to cut off scallion greens, leaving roots, white bulb, and 2 to 3 inches light green part intact. Save scallion greens for another use.

2 Add about 2 inches water to drinking glass. Place scallion bulbs in water, root end down (top of light green part should be sticking out of water). Put glass in sunny location.

3 Every day, discard the water from glass and replace with fresh water.

4 Watch your scallions grow! When scallion greens have grown 5 to 7 inches above white and light green parts (after about 1 week), use chef's knife to remove new scallion greens, leaving roots, white bulb, and 2 to 3 inches light green part intact. Use those scallion greens in a recipe!

5 If desired, repeat steps 2 through 4 to regrow and harvest scallion greens again. You can regrow a single scallion 2 times.

Notes
Use this space to write or draw your observations from this activity.

Regrowing Garlic

Don't throw away leftover garlic cloves either—grow garlic greens instead! Garlic greens taste similar to chives and scallions. You can use them the same way.

Here's how to do it:

1 Add ½ inch water to small glass or shallow container.

2 Place leftover unpeeled garlic cloves in water with root end (the flat part) facing down.

3 Replace water daily.

4 When garlic greens are 5 to 7 inches tall (after about 1 week), use chef's knife to remove greens.

Food for Thought

Scallions, sometimes called green onions, are part of a group of vegetables called alliums ("al-ee-ums"). They're related to garlic, onions, chives, and leeks. The white part of the scallion grows underground and stores nutrients for the rest of the plant— the light and dark green parts—that grows above ground.

The scallion roots absorb water. That water, plus energy from the sun and nutrients stored in the scallion white, helps grow a new scallion green—fast! The greens can grow as much as 1 inch per day! A scallion white contains enough nutrients to regrow scallion greens two more times before the plant runs out of fuel. Just think, you're getting three scallions for the price of one!

Awesome AVOCADOS and Amazing ACIDS

TOTAL TIME 5 minutes, plus 8–24 hours waiting time

Sometimes you need only part of an avocado for your taco or toast. But if you save the rest for later, your avocado will turn brown (oh no!). Can you keep it fresh and green? Find out in this easy experiment. If you don't have a whole lemon, use 3 tablespoons of bottled lemon juice.

Materials

1 lemon

1 cup water

1 ripe avocado

Chef's knife

Cutting board

Small bowl

Soupspoon

Small plate

Get Started!

1 Use chef's knife to cut lemon in half crosswise (not through ends). Rinse and dry knife.

2 Squeeze juice from lemon halves into small bowl. Add water to bowl.

3 Use knife to cut avocado in half lengthwise around pit. Using your hands, twist both halves in opposite directions to separate. Use soupspoon to scoop out pit. Discard pit.

4 Place 1 avocado half, cut side down, in bowl with lemon juice mixture. Place second avocado half on small plate, cut side up. Set bowl and plate in a spot where they won't be disturbed.

5 **Make a prediction:** What do you think each avocado half will look like after 8 hours? Will they look the same? Different? How so?

6 Let avocado halves sit for at least 8 hours and up to 24 hours.

7 Observe your results: Turn over avocado half in lemon juice mixture. Observe the 2 avocado halves. Do they look the same? Different? What do you notice about them?

8 Eat your experiment: Both avocado halves are safe to eat—use a spoon to gently scrape off any brown parts (the flesh underneath should be green). Will you use the avocado to make guacamole or avocado toast? Will you cut it up and use it on tacos or salad?

Notes Use this space to write or draw your observations from this experiment.

UNDERSTANDING YOUR RESULTS

Don't read until you've finished the experiment!

When you cut open an avocado, air touches the green flesh inside. After a few hours, the green avocado starts to turn brown—yuck!

Why does this happen? It comes down to chemistry: Molecules inside the avocado flesh react with oxygen in the air. That reaction, called oxidation ("ox-ih-DAY-shun"), creates new brown-colored molecules.

How can you stop cut avocados from turning brown? Acid to the rescue! Acids are found in ingredients such as lemon juice, lime juice, and vinegar. They are a kind of molecule called an antioxidant ("ann-tee-OX-ih-dent"). "Anti" means "against" and "oxi" means "oxygen," so antioxidants are molecules that help prevent the oxidation reaction that turns avocados brown.

Keeping the avocado flesh under water also helps prevent too much oxygen from touching it. That's why this combination of water and lemon juice works so well to keep the avocado green.

Design Challenge:
KEEP YOUR COOL

TOTAL TIME 45 minutes

On hot days, it's important to keep food and drinks cool. Not only will they taste better, but keeping food cold also helps prevent harmful microbes from growing. Your challenge? Design a container that keeps food cold, using materials you have at home.

Materials

2 small containers with lids, both made of the same material, such as plastic containers, cardboard boxes, or jars

Scissors

2 ice cubes

Here's a list of materials you could use for your designs, but feel free to use any supplies you have around your house! Aluminum foil • Cotton balls • Waxed paper • Scrap paper • Fabric scraps • Cardboard • String • Rubber bands • Newspaper • Paper towels • Bubble wrap • Tape • Glue

Get Started!

1 **Gather information:** A small container will be your base. You'll decide what materials to put inside of the container to keep it cold in

there—this is known as insulation ("in-suhl-AY-shun"). After you build your design, you'll test it by putting an ice cube inside of the container for 30 minutes and seeing how much it melts compared to an ice cube without insulation.

Think about other things you've seen that keep food cold on the go, such as lunch boxes, coolers, and thermoses. What properties do they have?

2 **Brainstorm your design:** What materials will you use for your insulation? Think about:

- Do you want a material that is thick? Thin? Fluffy? Hard?

- What are different ways you could use a material? For example, you can pull cotton balls apart into different shapes.

Sketch It Out Use this space to draw ideas for your design.

> [blank box for sketching]

3 **Build your design:** Place your insulation materials inside 1 container, leaving room for the ice cube. Will you add any insulation to the lid of the container?

4 **Test your design:** Place 1 ice cube inside container with your insulation. Place second ice cube inside second container (without insulation). Cover containers with lids. Set containers aside in a warm, sunny location for 30 minutes.

5 **Observe your results:** After 30 minutes, remove ice cubes from both containers. Which ice cube is larger? The larger ice cube melted less—it stayed cooler. Did your design keep the ice cube cooler than the container without insulation?

Notes Use this space to draw a picture of your final design. Label the parts.

> [blank box for drawing]

Food for Thought

Ice cubes in a glass melt a lot faster than ice cubes inside a thermos or cooler. Why? The biggest difference between a glass and a thermos is **insulation**. Insulation is any material that slows the movement of heat—it helps keep cold things cold (and hot things hot). Heat in the air moves more slowly through the insulation in the walls of the thermos than it does through the walls of the glass, which means the ice cubes stay colder and melt more slowly inside the thermos.

Why is that? One of the best insulation materials is **air**. Heat moves slowly through air, especially when the air is trapped inside of another material. Think about a cozy down jacket—a layer of fluffy down between two layers of fabric. Little pockets of air trapped inside the down slow the movement of heat from your warm body into the colder surrounding air.

Materials with air trapped inside, such as foam, are often good insulators. The walls of thermoses and coolers are often made of a hard plastic shell surrounding a layer of foam insulation. But you can also trap air using other materials: Shredded, crumpled, or fluffy materials create pockets of trapped air that slow the movement of heat.

Test out different insulation materials in your design. Which ones are best at keeping the inside of the container—and the ice cube—cool?

CHILL OUT

TOTAL TIME 5 minutes, plus 4 hours freezing time before you begin the experiment

Do all frozen things feel equally cold? Melt your mind with this surprising sensory experiment.

Materials

1 ice cube

2-tablespoon cube of butter

2 zipper-lock bags

Get Started!

1 **At least 4 hours before you want to do this experiment**, place ice cube in zipper-lock bag, seal bag (remove as much air as possible), and place bag in the freezer. Place 2-tablespoon cube of butter in second zipper-lock bag, seal bag (remove as much air as possible), and place that bag in the freezer, too.

2 **Make a prediction**: When you take the ice cube and butter out of the freezer and hold them in your hands:

- Will the butter feel colder than the ice cube?

- Will the ice cube feel colder than the butter?

- Will they feel the same?

3 After at least 4 hours, take bags out of freezer. Keeping them in their bags, hold ice cube in one hand and cube of frozen butter in your other hand for 15 to 30 seconds. (To make this experiment as scientific as possible, close your eyes and have an adult or a friend place one bag in each of your hands. This is called a blind test because you can't see the samples and you don't know which is which.)

4 **Observe your results:** Does one cube feel colder than the other, or do they feel the same?

Notes Use this space to write or draw your observations from this experiment.

STOP

UNDERSTANDING YOUR RESULTS

Don't read until you've finished the experiment!

Whoa—that was weird, right? When we tried this experiment in the America's Test Kitchen Kids lab, everyone agreed that the ice cube felt WAY colder than the frozen butter. But how can that be? The butter and the ice cube were in the same freezer, and when we measured their temperatures, they were both 3 degrees. What's going on?

Things feel cold to us when heat is removed from our bodies. Heat always moves from warmer things, like your hand, to colder things, such as the frozen butter or ice cube. The movement of heat energy out of your body is what makes you feel cold.

But why does the ice cube (frozen water) feel colder in your hand than the frozen butter?

It's because water needs a LOT of heat energy to warm up. Butter, which is made of about 80 percent fat and only about 15 percent water, needs much less energy

to warm up the same amount. Here's one way to think about it:

Say you and a friend each have a bucket you want to fill up with water. Your bucket is a lot bigger than your friend's bucket, so you need a lot more water (and time!) to fill it to the top. You're like water! Your friend, who fills up their bucket quickly, with less water, is like butter.

To get water (or ice) hot, you need to fill up a big bucket with heat energy. To get the same amount of butter to the same hotness, you need to fill up only a small bucket with heat energy.

In our experiment, that heat energy comes from your warm hands. A lot of heat energy has to move from your hand to the ice to warm it up—that makes your hand feel very cold. Warming the frozen butter takes a lot less heat energy from your hand, so your hand doesn't feel quite as cold.

How to Make the BEST WHIPPED CREAM EVER

MAKES About 2 cups whipped cream
TOTAL TIME 30 minutes

In this experiment, discover the secret to making the lightest, fluffiest whipped cream. You can substitute whipping cream for the heavy cream, but do NOT substitute light cream or half-and-half. An electric mixer will give you the fastest results. You can use a whisk to whip the cream by hand—be prepared for a workout! It will take about twice as long.

Materials

½ cup plus ½ cup cold heavy cream, measured separately

1½ teaspoons plus 1½ teaspoons sugar, measured separately

½ teaspoon plus ½ teaspoon vanilla extract, measured separately

Masking tape or sticky notes

Marker or pen

2 equal-size clear, tall drinking glasses

Liquid measuring cup

Instant-read thermometer (optional)

2 medium bowls

Electric mixer

Rubber spatula

2 spoons per person

Get Started!

1 **Make a prediction:** In this experiment, you'll explore whether the temperature of heavy cream affects the fluffiness of whipped cream. (Heavy cream is the main ingredient in whipped cream.) Which do you predict will make fluffier whipped cream, **cold** heavy cream or **room-temperature** heavy cream?

2 Use masking tape and marker to label 1 drinking glass "Room Temperature" and second drinking glass "Cold." Set aside.

3 Measure ½ cup cold heavy cream, straight from refrigerator. Pour cold heavy cream into medium bowl. (If you have an instant-read thermometer, take the temperature of the heavy cream—it should be about 40 degrees.)

4 Add 1½ teaspoons sugar and ½ teaspoon vanilla to bowl with cold heavy cream. Use electric mixer on medium-low speed to whip cream for about 1 minute. Increase speed to high and whip until cream is smooth and thick, about 1 minute. Stop mixer and lift beaters out of cream. If whipped cream clings to beaters and makes soft peaks that stand up on their own, you're done! If not, keep beating and check again in 30 seconds.

5 Use rubber spatula to gently scoop whipped cream into drinking glass labeled "Cold." Use spatula to gently smooth top. Set glass aside.

6 Clean beaters and rubber spatula before you whip second batch of heavy cream.

7 Measure remaining ½ cup heavy cream into liquid measuring cup. Heat in microwave at 50 percent power in 10-second increments for about 20 seconds, or until cream registers about 70 degrees on instant-read thermometer. (If you don't have an instant-read thermometer, the heavy cream should feel neutral to the touch, neither warm nor cold.)

8 In clean medium bowl, combine room-temperature heavy cream, remaining sugar, and remaining vanilla. Use electric mixer on medium-low speed to whip cream for about 1 minute. Increase speed to high and whip until cream is smooth and thick, about 1 minute. Stop mixer and lift beaters out of cream. If whipped cream clings to beaters and makes soft peaks that stand up on their own, you're done! If not, keep beating and check again in 30 seconds.

turn the page!

It's possible that the room-temperature heavy cream will not reach soft peaks, especially if you are using pasteurized heavy cream instead of ultrapasteurized heavy cream. If you've whipped the cream for 2 minutes and 30 seconds and it still has not reached soft peaks, stop and continue to step 9.

9   Use rubber spatula to gently scoop whipped cream into drinking glass labeled "Room Temperature." Use spatula to gently smooth top.

10 **Observe your results:** Compare your 2 batches of whipped cream:

- Which one fills up more of the drinking glass, the whipped cream made from cold heavy cream or the whipped cream made from room-temperature heavy cream?

- How do your results compare with your preduction?

11 Time for a taste test! Be sure to use a clean spoon for each taste.

- Do the 2 batches of whipped cream taste the same or different?

- Are their textures the same or different? How so?

12 Use your whipped cream to top your favorite desserts, or dollop it on top of fresh fruit.

Want to use your whipped cream a little later?

It will keep in a bowl in the refrigerator for up to 1 hour. If you want to store it for up to 8 hours, spoon the whipped cream into a fine-mesh strainer set over a medium bowl. Place the fine-mesh strainer and bowl in the refrigerator until you're ready to use the whipped cream. Over time, whipped cream releases liquid. This is called "weeping." Putting the whipped cream in the fine-mesh strainer lets the liquid drain into the bowl below and keeps your whipped cream fluffy, not watery.

Notes Use this space to write or draw your observations from this experiment.

 STOP ⟩ UNDERSTANDING YOUR RESULTS

Don't read until you've finished the experiment!

When we tried this experiment in the America's Test Kitchen Kids lab, the whipped cream made from cold heavy cream was light and fluffy and had nearly twice the volume of the whipped cream made from room-temperature cream. Did your experiment turn out the same way?

Why is temperature so important to making fluffy, cloud-like whipped cream?

First, we have to understand how whipped cream works. Heavy cream is made of 36 to 40 percent fat (the rest is water, protein, sugars, and minerals). The big difference between liquid heavy cream and whipped heavy cream is air— the sugar and vanilla extract add only sweetness and flavor. Whipping heavy cream using an electric mixture or by hand creates lots of tiny air bubbles. The fat in the cream holds the air bubbles in place. As more and more air bubbles form,

the heavy cream expands and becomes light and fluffy.

And here's where temperature comes in: As fat warms up, say from refrigerator temperature (about 40 degrees) to room temperature (about 70 degrees), it gets softer. Think about gently squeezing a stick of butter straight from the fridge versus one you've left out for a couple of hours. The room-temperature butter is softer and easier to squeeze, while the cold butter holds its shape.

The warmer, softer fat in the room-temperature heavy cream can't support the air bubbles very well, so they start to collapse. That means the finished whipped cream won't have as much volume. The fat in the cold heavy cream is more solid, so it can support more trapped air bubbles— this makes for fluffier whipped cream with more volume.

Bubbly
BAKING

TOTAL TIME 20 minutes

Baking soda and baking powder are both chemical leaveners—they create bubbly carbon dioxide gas that helps baked goods such as muffins, cakes, and quick breads rise without needing to use yeast. In this experiment, you'll find out the difference between these two ingredients and learn how they work their bubbly science! Any type of vinegar will work in this experiment.

Materials

1 teaspoon baking powder

1 teaspoon baking soda

¼ cup plus ¼ cup water, measured separately

1 teaspoon vinegar

Masking tape or sticky notes

Marker or pen

2 clear, tall drinking glasses

Get Started!

1 Use masking tape and marker to label 1 drinking glass "Baking Powder" and second drinking glass "Baking Soda."

2 Add baking powder to glass labeled "Baking Powder." Add baking soda to glass labeled "Baking Soda."

3 **Make a prediction:** What do you think will happen when you add water to the baking powder and baking soda?

4 Place both glasses in sink. Pour ¼ cup water into each glass.

5 **Observe your results:** What happened when you added water to each glass? Did you see any bubbles of carbon dioxide gas?

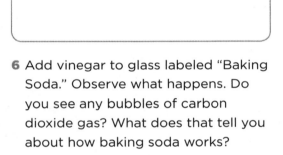

6 Add vinegar to glass labeled "Baking Soda." Observe what happens. Do you see any bubbles of carbon dioxide gas? What does that tell you about how baking soda works?

STOP ▸ UNDERSTANDING YOUR RESULTS

Don't read until you've finished the experiment!

Lots of baking recipes call for baking powder, baking soda, or both. When baking soda comes in contact with an acid, such as the vinegar in this experiment, it creates bubbly carbon dioxide gas. In recipes that use baking soda, you'll almost always see an acidic ingredient, like lemon juice, lime juice, buttermilk, or even yogurt. Baking powder, on the other hand, already contains an acid—and it actually contains baking soda, too. It only needs a liquid (in this experiment, we used water) to start creating carbon dioxide gas.

In recipes for baked goods, such as muffins, quick breads, and cakes, the bubbly carbon dioxide gas causes the batter to rise in the oven, giving the finished product its height and a light, fluffy texture.

Notes Use this space to write or draw your observations from this experiment.

Sketch Imagine there's a superhero chef—draw what they look like (and what they cook) on this page!

CHAPTER 3 Games and Puzzles!

Pasta

Can you find these 10 pasta-rific words hidden in the puzzle? Look for them across, down, and diagonally!

```
F M I N I U F T K G Z L Z U L Z Z F J M
B V U A B G F Z X H Q O C T I R Y O R N
F S F O A V Q W X Y Y V F T N P V W Z N
P L N A Z W U Z X B G K P J G B S N N S
T V A J R C W C R B W Z H W U P Z V F M
D B Z B Z F I O J Y M X O X I Y O I W N
D U E U U A A P W V O T V D N L O S T N
R C L W F S L L H D M D A C E D C J R I
N A B S C U M Z L N V V K B Z B E N I A
F T O G G T B Y L E I P G B A I X W V M
J I W L D S P A G H E T T I V P W H Y G
F N S I A Q M O P K U Z C J O N G E H X
X I W G J P G D J L F I D Y E A C Q R Z
X I H B P Q O O U W I F F P Y G V G Y D
I O X V T G Y D F O A I K D Z U F F H Y
M X R S P X B R G A W W E I H K R K U Y
V T F Z J E H X J D S S H M B E S H I O
G H H W O A N R I G A T O N I I N V F C
P X C U Z Y N N R Q J R F U S I L L I E
G J R Q E G N Y E I I V X D R Z G K V V
```

SPAGHETTI **BUCATINI** **FARFALLE** **RIGATONI** **ORZO**
LINGUINE **ZITI** **FUSILLI** **PENNE** **ELBOWS**

Did you know that there are more than 1,300 different pasta shapes?!

Breakfast

Start your morning right and find these 12 breakfast-y words hidden in the puzzle. Look for them across, down, and diagonally!

```
G V D J W E U P H G T E K T R Z D O P N
E C T S A M D B K I G J O X T C E I V T
G Q D R F I B A F S A U S A G E B N S L
G W R N F O A T M E A L E V W T X H I S
S H C W L P R D H Y F Q F K P O N Q X N
W Y W K E C N O R U I S B V F A T A K T
I Y W P S X Y G Y O G U R T G S E L N O
K L R D D T L C C A C G O O B T H C P J
Z P J A K M X V H L V Q W X Y T N E V V
N O W R T P D S R S M X R I E G K R D E
D O U G H N U T S A D N J B Y X P E J A
O K N P D V T P G B B S P K F X N B W J
C X Y P R A Z S E S I N M C D B F N V J
S E G W A M U Y Z U Q N Q O E S S E R U
B O F L L N Y P C O W Y H U O R R W G I
O F T S Z W C N S D A Q J Q X T E E C C
H B R X P K P A I R B K X M W R H A B E
H L D N K N D G K N J F D D H M T I L J
E T Q F F T I A U E W Y F Z N V R O E V
K A K Y W C Z K S E S B B A C O N R M Q
```

PANCAKES	**EGGS**	**JUICE**	**DOUGHNUTS**
WAFFLES	**TOAST**	**BACON**	**YOGURT**
CEREAL	**OATMEAL**	**SAUSAGE**	**SMOOTHIE**

Who says you can only eat breakfast in the morning? I like to have breakfast for dinner!

Kitchen Tools

Use your eyes (handy tools built into your own head!) to find the 12 kitchen tools hidden in this puzzle. Look for them across, down, and diagonally!

```
G H S J H M U Y T G N K G R A T E R S A
W P R C T U W W L R K W Q O C C W G G T
V D K D E W Y T M K F X Q I O Q V Y K W
S R C G D Z A H M B N F M V V Y B F K R
E C P X Z C J N O M O I V Y C T K J S C
K G Z Z R G O F Z T Y A F F O G V M E O
J L Y L B B V L S V B W Y E C Z G B H X
S Z A B S O L Z A W D C M I A L X B E B
A M N D R W R M F N O I K S K I L L E T
U I K M L L A S L H D U U W A I J Y C T
C X R O S E H N X H Q E L R H V S V K H
E E W V A X S R X D X H R E X I B Q U V
P R K B C O B G V F U J P Y Q U S Q F R
A K M J N I H L Q J D W M F O G W K Q G
N K T X K E H X E N K K H E K K M P F S
A U O D A L B N U X H O O K F C J X Q M
G E N L I G S P A T U L A G D R Q N N Q
T Q G X L E B T J U N P C F V Q U Z R M
P L S C S O X E I C U F F N Y I A Z G M
F X Y C E V M C S P O O N Z P V B X I A
```

WHISK   **KNIFE**   **LADLE**

SPATULA   **TONGS**   **BOWL**

SKILLET   **COLANDER**   **SAUCEPAN**

MIXER   **GRATER**   **SPOON**

It's my time to shine! You can use a whisk (that's me!) for everything from making pancakes and salad dressing to whipping cream.

Cookies

Can you unscramble the letters in these jumbled words to reveal the names of 12 delicious cookies?

HATCOOLCE CIHP
_ _ _ _ _ _ _ _ _ _ _ _ _ _

LAEMOAT
_ _ _ _ _ _ _

SDLEDECRIKONO
_ _ _ _ _ _ _ _ _ _ _ _ _

MJA RBPMTTUINH
_ _ _ _ _ _ _ _ _ _ _

LOHCATCEO NEILKCR
_ _ _ _ _ _ _ _ _ _ _ _ _ _ _

IRBGARGEEND
_ _ _ _ _ _ _ _ _ _ _

UPTANE BRUTTE
_ _ _ _ _ _ _ _ _ _ _ _

GRASU OOIKEC
_ _ _ _ _ _ _ _ _ _ _

TORRSBEAHD
_ _ _ _ _ _ _ _ _ _

OSMALSSE
_ _ _ _ _ _ _ _

ONROMCAA
_ _ _ _ _ _ _ _

SCHDIWAN KOICOE
_ _ _ _ _ _ _ _ _ _ _ _ _ _

Desserts!

Exercise your mind with this dessert-centric crossword puzzle.

- You don't need to solve this puzzle in order—read through all the clues and start with the ones that are easiest for you.

- It can be fun to solve crossword puzzles with friends or family (plus, more people = more brain power!).

- Finally, crossword puzzle clues are not always straightforward—don't hesitate to think outside the box.

ACROSS

2 A "berry" delicious summertime dessert

3 A young Girl Scout or a chocolaty treat

5 A weighty dessert?

7 Pucker up for these bright yellow squares

9 An English person might think this fall dessert is made of potato chips

12 A famous New York dessert

DOWN

1 Milk's best friend

4 We all "scream" for it

6 A treat you can only enjoy on the weekend?

8 It's as easy as _____

10 A cold, fruity treat in the summertime

11 You might share them at a birthday party

SEE PAGE 132 FOR THE ANSWERS

Road Trip

First, ask your friends or family to come up with words to fill the blank spaces in this story. (Don't read the story out loud yet!) Write their words in the blank spaces. Encourage everyone to be as silly and creative as they can! After you've filled in all the blanks, read the (now very silly!) story out loud.

Parts of Speech:

NOUN
A word (such as sibling, cafe, or sandwich) for a person, place, or thing

ADJECTIVE
A word (such as sparkly, crispy, or tall) that describes a noun

VERB
A word (such as jump, eat, or chop) used to describe an action

PAST-TENSE VERB
A word (such as jumped, ate, or chopped) used to describe an action that has already happened

Mitsy was just about done packing for her annual road trip, and she could not have been more excited. It was another _____ day of
_{Adjective}
summer vacation, her favorite time of year to put the

_____ to the _____
Noun   Noun

and explore the open _____, as the
Noun

saying goes. But Mitsy had to make sure she'd packed everything she and her friends would need before they set out on this year's _____
Adjective

adventure!

She had packed plenty of _____
Food Item

in case they got hungry along the way. And she remembered to bring a _____ in
Noun

case they got bored. She even had her favorite stuffed _____ in case she got
Noun

homesick. But what was she forgetting? THE MAP!

Mitsy had planned the most _____ road trip, and she

had every stop laid out on that map. She couldn't _____
_____ Verb

without it! Good thing she remembered putting it behind the

_____ in the recipe lab fridge, which is where she
_____ Noun

keeps all her most _____ possessions.
_____ Adjective

They were going to start by visiting _____'s
_____ Person in Room

Castle, the largest structure made out of _____ on this
_____ Noun

continent. Then they'd _____ south to see the world's
_____ Verb

_____-est ball of _____, which
_____ Adjective _____ Noun

may as well have been the eighth Wonder of the World. After that, they'd

drive past the _____ Canyon on the way to
_____ Adjective

_____-wood Forest and stop for tea and
_____ Adjective

_____ at Queen Victoria's _____
_____ Plural Noun _____ Noun

before they reached the coast.

Misty loved the coast the most. She couldn't wait to lay out a beach towel,

_____ a _____ back and forth with her
_____ Verb _____ Noun

friends, and watch the sunset across the _____ water.
_____ Adjective

She could almost taste the _____ they'd roast on the
_____ Plural Noun

campfire. BUT, first things first! Mitsy went to go pack the map.

You can hear more of my adventures in our kid-friendly podcast, *Mystery Recipe*! Listen wherever you get your podcasts.

Holiday Adventure

First, ask your friends or family to come up with words to fill the blank spaces in this story. Write their words in the blank spaces. Encourage everyone to be as silly and creative as they can! After you've filled in all the blanks, read the (now very silly!) story out loud. (See page 106 for definitions of the parts of speech.)

"HAPPY NATIONAL HAND-HOLDING DAY!" Mitsy sang out as she

_____ down the stair's handrail and into the recipe lab.
Past Tense Verb

"Might I enlighten you with a _____ history of National
Adjective

Hand-Holding Day while we _____ our customary breakfast
Verb

bagels?" she asked her friends.

"It all started _____ years ago, in a town just outside of
Number

_____. It was a _____ summer day, and
Place   Adjective

our hero, the baker, was busy doing what they did every day: making

bagels for their town to enjoy for breakfast. They had a _____
Adjective

oven outside of their home, and this morning they were really in the groove.

They'd _____ and _____ each bagel and,
Verb   Verb

with a flick of the wrist, into the oven they'd go. Finally, all the bagels

were in the oven. The baker was waiting for the _____
Adjective

bagels to bake, but they were getting bored, so they'd balance their

spatula on their finger and flip it up into the air. But then they threw the

spatula a bit too high! A seagull, flying past and thinking they'd spotted a

_____ morning snack, _____
  Adjective   Past Tense Verb

down, grabbed the spatula, and flew away.

The bagels were almost ready and the entire town was _____
                                                                              Adjective

and lining up for food. How would the baker get the bagels out of the oven?!

They couldn't just _____ in and grab the tray—it was too hot!
                            Verb

"I have a _____ idea," said a voice behind the baker.
                  Adjective

The baker turned around to see . . . their warm winter mittens?

"Mittens!" the baker shouted with _____. "It's the middle
                                                    Emotion

of summer, and these bagels are about to _____ ! This is no
                                                            Verb

time for you!"

"Well, in the _____ winter I may keep your
                      Adjective

_____ warm, this is true, but perhaps I can protect
  Plural Noun

your hands from the heat of the oven today."

And on that day, the oven mitt was born. It took a few _____
                                                                          Adjective

years to get the type of mitt you know and love today, but every year, on

the hottest day of summer, we wear our winter mittens and eat bagels to

celebrate that _____ first mitt's willingness to hold a hand.
                      Adjective

Happy National Hand-Holding Day, everyone!

You can hear more of Mitsy's adventures in our kid-friendly podcast, *Mystery Recipe*! Listen wherever you get your podcasts.

Busting Kitchen Myths

Some cooking tips have been passed down for generations—but that doesn't necessarily mean that they're true. Many of these tips don't actually work. They might sound like "facts," but science tells us that they are myths. (We've tested them all out!) Can you figure out which statements are facts and which are myths?

1 ☐ MYTH or ☐ FACT
Covering your pot will make the water boil faster.

2 ☐ MYTH or ☐ FACT
Slamming the oven door or stomping your feet in the kitchen while a cake is baking will cause your cake to sink disastrously in the middle.

3 ☐ MYTH or ☐ FACT
You should never wash fresh mushrooms.

4 ☐ MYTH or ☐ FACT
Adding oil to pasta cooking water will keep the pasta from sticking.

5 ☐ MYTH or ☐ FACT
Searing a steak in a pan over high heat is the best way to seal in its delicious juices.

6 ☐ MYTH or ☐ FACT
You can regrow scallions by putting the roots in a glass of water, even if you've used up the green parts.

SEE PAGE 133 FOR THE ANSWERS

Fruit or Vegetable?

Is a tomato a fruit or a vegetable? The answer might surprise you. We often call tomatoes vegetables because they're eaten in savory dishes. But if you think about it from the perspective of the tomato plant, a tomato is most definitely a FRUIT.

Fruits form from a flower's ovary and always contain seeds. They tend to be juicy and sweet so that animals want to eat them, and then the animals spread the seeds through—you guessed it—their poop. Vegetables, on the other hand, are all the other parts of a plant that we eat, such as the leaves, stems, roots, and even the flowers! Now that you've got the scoop on fruit, see if you can figure out whether each of these foods is a fruit or a vegetable. *Lettuce* begin!

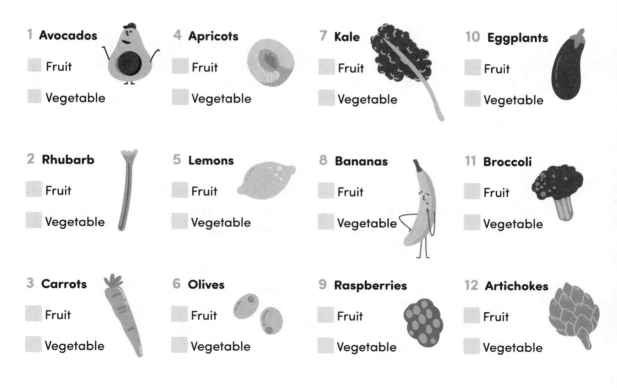

1 Avocados
- Fruit
- Vegetable

2 Rhubarb
- Fruit
- Vegetable

3 Carrots
- Fruit
- Vegetable

4 Apricots
- Fruit
- Vegetable

5 Lemons
- Fruit
- Vegetable

6 Olives
- Fruit
- Vegetable

7 Kale
- Fruit
- Vegetable

8 Bananas
- Fruit
- Vegetable

9 Raspberries
- Fruit
- Vegetable

10 Eggplants
- Fruit
- Vegetable

11 Broccoli
- Fruit
- Vegetable

12 Artichokes
- Fruit
- Vegetable

SEE PAGE 133 FOR THE ANSWERS

Cheese!

Humans have been making cheese for thousands of years. The process always starts with milk (cow's milk of course, but also goat's, sheep's, buffalo's, yak's, and even camel's milk!). Depending on how cheese is made, it can have many different flavors and textures: hard, soft, smooth, crumbly, creamy, tangy, sweet, nutty, and many more. Grab your suitcase and see if you can figure out which country each of these cheeses comes from.

1 **Cheddar cheese** is made from cow's milk and has been around for more than 900 years (!). It was invented in a village called Cheddar in this country, which is also famous for foods such as Yorkshire pudding, fish and chips, and bubble and squeak:

    A. Switzerland   C. Australia

    B. England   D. Japan

2 Nutty, salty, savory **Parmigiano-Reggiano** is a hard, dense cheese made from cow's milk. It is often grated over dishes, such as pasta or risotto. It comes from:

    A. Italy   C. India

    B. Spain   D. Finland

3 **Feta cheese** is traditionally made from sheep's milk and is stored in a salty liquid called a brine. Feta is crumbly and has a salty, tangy flavor. Feta originated in this country, which also created the Olympic games and the Parthenon:

    A. Brazil   C. Morocco

    B. South Korea   D. Greece

4 Ooh la la! Gooey, buttery **Brie** ("bree") is a soft cheese with a firm, white rind and a creamy interior. Brie traditionally hails from this European country:

    A. Ireland   C. France

    B. Croatia   D. Norway

5 **Cotija** ("ko-TEE-hah") is a hard, salty, white cheese made from cow's milk. Cotija doesn't really melt—it's traditionally crumbled on top of dishes, such as tacos, enchiladas, and black beans. It comes from this North American country:

    A. Mexico   C. Jamaica

    B. United States   D. Canada

6 **Paneer** ("pah-NEAR") is what's known as a fresh cheese—it isn't aged at all. Paneer has a mild flavor and a slightly chewy texture. It's often cooked in the cuisine of this Asian country, which has the second-highest population in the world (1.2 billion people) and 22 official languages (the most popular is Hindi).

    A. Japan   C. India

    B. Indonesia   D. Thailand

Food Lingo

Cooking has its own language. It might seem like a foreign language—but luckily you don't have to learn too many new words. Can you figure out which cooking word is being described in the definition?

1 ☐ **SIMMER or** ☐ **SAUTÉ**

To heat a liquid until small bubbles gently break the surface at a variable and infrequent rate.

2 ☐ **STEAM or** ☐ **SWEAT**

To cook food over gentle heat, in a small amount of fat, in a covered pot.

3 ☐ **FRY or** ☐ **POACH**

To cook food in hot water or other liquid that is held below the simmering point.

4 ☐ **BOIL or** ☐ **BROIL**

To heat a liquid until large bubbles break the surface at a rapid and constant rate.

5 ☐ **SEAR or** ☐ **SCRAMBLE**

To cook food over high heat, without moving it in the pan, with the goal of creating a deeply browned crust.

6 ☐ **SLICE or** ☐ **DICE**

To cut food into uniform cubes (the exact size depends on the recipe).

7 ☐ **FOLD or** ☐ **PEEL**

To mix delicate batters and incorporate fragile ingredients using a gentle under-and-over motion that minimizes deflation.

8 ☐ **TOAST or** ☐ **GRATE**

To cook or brown food (especially nuts or bread crumbs) using dry heat and without adding fat.

9 ☐ **KNEAD or** ☐ **CHOP**

To cut food into small pieces (⅛ inch to ¾ inch, depending on the recipe).

SEE PAGE 133 FOR THE ANSWERS GAMES AND PUZZLES!

In the Test Kitchen

Can you find and circle the 12 differences between these two pictures?!

Desert Island

Imagine: You're going to go live on a desert island alone for one full month. You won't be in danger, and you won't go hungry. But you will have to make some culinary sacrifices. Talk through these decisions with family or friends. Will you make the same—or different—choices?

Would you rather eat ALL fruit or ALL vegetables for the month?

. . . have only cake or only pie for dessert?

. . . eat warm ice cream or cold pizza for every meal?

. . . eat all breakfasts or all dinners?

. . . bring a skillet or a knife?

. . . bring a whisk or a rubber spatula?

. . . have access to salt or hot sauce?

. . . cook with only an oven or only a grill?

. . . bring only a spoon or only a fork?

. . . bring only cookies or only crackers for snacking?

. . . bring bread or cheese (but not both!)?

You can only bring one DINNER. What will it be?

You can bring one DESSERT. What will it be?

Use this space to write down your top THREE foods to bring to the island.

Use this space to write down your top THREE drinks to bring to the island.

Use this space to write down your top THREE cooking tools to bring to the island.

Condiment Madness!

Condiments aren't sports teams . . . but they're pretty close, right? Use this bracket to pit your favorite condiments against one another. We know, we know, you wouldn't use all these condiments on the same food. Think of it more like you're going to go live on that desert island (see left) and can only bring the CHAMPION condiment with you!

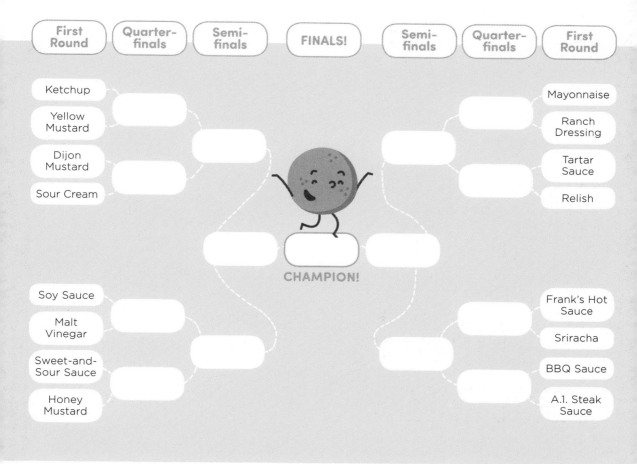

First Round	Quarter-finals	Semi-finals	FINALS!	Semi-finals	Quarter-finals	First Round
Ketchup						Mayonnaise
Yellow Mustard						Ranch Dressing
Dijon Mustard						Tartar Sauce
Sour Cream						Relish
			CHAMPION!			
Soy Sauce						Frank's Hot Sauce
Malt Vinegar						Sriracha
Sweet-and-Sour Sauce						BBQ Sauce
Honey Mustard						A.1. Steak Sauce

Doughnuts, Tacos, Ice Cream, & Pies

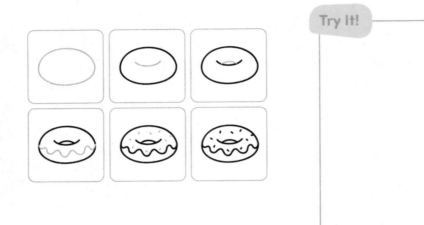

Try It!

Try It!

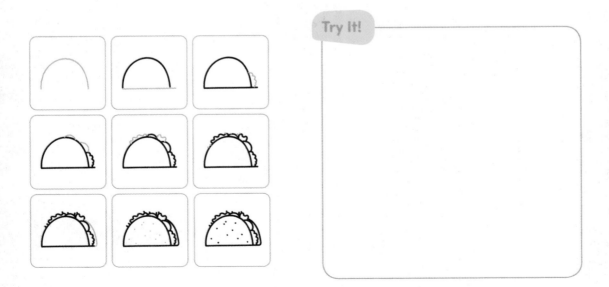

The Name Game

Test your knowledge of food names! Play this trivia game by yourself or with your family or friends.

1 Plum, cherry, and Roma are types of what?

A. Grapes

B. Tomatoes

C. Potatoes

2 Basmati and jasmine are types of what grain?

A. Corn

B. Quinoa

C. Rice

3 Xigua is another name for what fruit?

A. Watermelon

B. Banana

C. Mango

4 What is another name for scallions?

A. Green onions

B. Onion sticks

C. Long onions

5 Snow and sugar snap are types of what vegetable?

A. Corn

B. Lettuce

C. Pea

6 Red, white, and Vidalia are types of what?

A. Onions

B. Apples

C. Peppers

7 Kidney, lima, and pinto are types of what?

A. Greens

B. Beans

C. Pasta

8 Pitaya is another name for what fruit?

A. Dragon fruit

B. Blueberry

C. Cantaloupe

9 Sesame, chia, and flax are all edible what?

A. Grains

B. Nuts

C. Seeds

10 Cobblers and buckles are two types of what?

A. Breakfast cereals

B. Casserole dishes

C. Fruit desserts

11 Farfalle, ziti, and penne are types of what?

A. Pasta

B. Herbs

C. Grains

12 Dried grapes are better known as what?

A. Fruit leather

B. Jerky

C. Raisins

13 Trumpet, enoki, and button are types of what?

A. Beans

B. Squash

C. Mushrooms

14 Nori, kelp, and dulse are types of what?

A. Edible seaweed

B. Kale

C. Herbs

15 What are baby portobello mushrooms called?

A. Shiitake mushrooms

B. Mushettes

C. Cremini mushrooms

SEE PAGE 134 FOR THE ANSWERS

What's It Made From?

What ingredients go into your favorite foods? Play this trivia game by yourself or with your family or friends.

1 **What is polenta made from?**
A. Bee pollen
B. Ground cornmeal
C. Whole wheat

2 **What are most tortilla chips made from?**
A. Wheat
B. Rice
C. Corn

3 **What is miso made from?**
A. Sesame seeds
B. Fermented soybeans
C. Fruit juice

4 **What is caramel made from?**
A. Melted, browned sugar
B. Thickened cream
C. Heated milk and honey

5 **What is tahini made from?**
A. Ground-up roasted peanuts
B. Ground-up chickpeas
C. Ground-up toasted sesame seeds

6 **What is half-and-half made of?**
A. Half milk, half cream
B. Half butter, half milk
C. Half yogurt, half cream

7 **Kimchi and sauerkraut are made from what?**
A. Onions
B. Cabbage
C. Celery

8 **What is the main ingredient in hummus?**
A. Potatoes
B. White beans
C. Chickpeas

9 **What is cinnamon made from?**
A. The petals of a flower
B. The dried berries of a vine plant
C. The bark of a tree

10 **What are cheese and yogurt made from?**
A. Milk
B. Butter
C. Water

11 **What is the main ingredient in mayonnaise?**
A. Oil
B. Cream
C. Butter

12 **What is butter made from?**
A. Oil
B. Cream
C. Cheese

SEE PAGE 135 FOR THE ANSWERS

Ingredient Investigation

Take a walk through an imaginary grocery store . . . and answer some trivia along the way. Play this trivia game by yourself or with your family or friends.

1 Pummelo, satsuma, and clementines are types of what?

A. Pumpkins

B. Cheeses

C. Citrus fruits

2 Basil, cilantro, and thyme are types of what?

A. Herbs

B. Fruits

C. Weeds

3 What's another word for grated citrus peel?

A. Pith

B. Skin

C. Zest

4 What part of the broccoli plant do we eat?

A. The leaves

B. The flower buds

C. The root

5 What are the yellow specks on a strawberry?

A. Seeds

B. Pollen

C. Fungus

6 What vegetable is called "maíz" in Spanish?

A. Beans

B. Corn

C. Peppers

7 Where does black pepper come from?

A. The dried berries of a vine plant

B. The seeds of a tree

C. Dried bell peppers

8 Soba, udon, and ramen are types of what?

A. Noodles

B. Rice

C. Flours

9 Which takes longer to cook?

A. Brown rice

B. White rice

C. They take the same amount of time to cook

10 Peewee, large, and jumbo are sizes of what?

A. Containers of yogurt

B. Blocks of cheese

C. Chicken eggs

11 "Milk" and "dark" are two types of what?

A. Ice cream

B. Chocolate

C. Cheese

12 What makes blue cheese blue?

A. Mold

B. Food coloring

C. Spices

13 Cake, bread, and all-purpose are types of what?

A. Baked goods

B. Desserts

C. Flours

14 What are baking powder and baking soda?

A. Flours

B. Spices

C. Leaveners

15 What is a vanilla bean?

A. The stem of a tropical plant

B. The seed pod of an orchid flower

C. The root of a fruit tree

Your Dream Dinner

Close your eyes. Imagine your ideal dinner. It can be anything you want. Steak, potatoes, and green beans? A unicorn cake and cotton candy? Draw it here and label the different parts.

Give your dish a name!

Kitchen Edition!

Ready for the best-ever version of I Spy? Take a look around your kitchen—in the pantry, cupboards, drawers, refrigerator, and freezer. Can you find objects, foods, or ingredients that match each of the descriptions below? Write what you find in the blank spaces. You can play this game by yourself or together with family and friends.

Something **green**

Something **blue**

Something **yellow**

Something **red**

Something **orange**

Something **black**

Something **white**

Something **purple**

Something **brown**

Something **metal**

Something **glass**

Something **plastic**

Something **wooden**

Something **smaller than your hand**

Something **bigger than your body**

Something **round**

The taste of umami ("oo-MA-me") is meaty or savory. Some foods with a lot of umami taste are tomatoes, mushrooms, miso, soy sauce, Parmesan cheese, and meats.

Something **umami**

Something **bitter**

Something **salty**

Something **sour**

Something **sweet**

Something **flat**

Something **transparent**

Something **rough**

Something **loud**

Something **quiet**

Something **from nature**

Something **made by humans**

Something **solid**

Something **liquid**

Something **sharp**

Something **square**

Something **shiny**

Something **hard**

Something **soft**

Something **spicy**

Something **hot**

Something **cold**

Something **dry**

Something **wet**

Food Truck

Imagine that you're a chef about to open your own food truck. What would you call it? Would it have a theme? What would you put on the menu? Use the space below to capture your creative, delicious ideas!

What will you name your food truck?

Draw your food truck logo here.

A logo is a picture or design that represents your food truck.

What will your food truck look like? What color will it be? Will you have a menu on the outside? Tables nearby for people to sit at? Draw and color your ideas below.

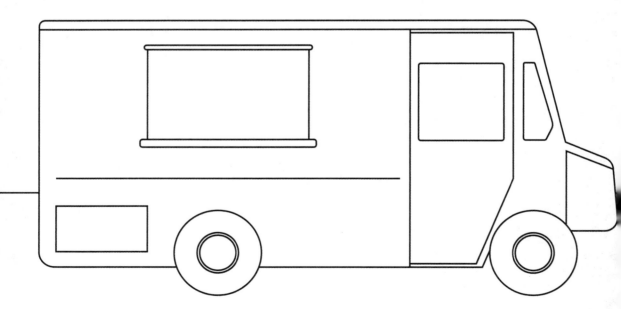

When you're naming dishes on your menu, it's fun to include adjectives that describe the way the dish tastes or looks, such as crispy, fresh, juicy, sweet, spicy, or tangy. Creamy mac and cheese sounds tastier than plain old mac and cheese, right? You can even add your name to show that something is your signature dish!

Make Your Menu

What will you serve from your food truck? How many different dishes will you have on the menu? Write them in the menu template below.

MAIN DISHES

SIDE DISHES

DRINKS

DESSERTS

Limericks

Poetry is a form of writing that makes you feel something through carefully chosen words. You can write a rhyming poem (or not), a funny poem, a love poem, or . . . a poem about your favorite food! Even though you can write poetry without any set structure (that's called free verse poetry), sometimes it's helpful to have some guidelines. Use this space to create your own limerick about your favorite foods.

A **limerick** is five lines long, and usually silly. The first, second, and fifth lines all rhyme, and each line should contain 7 to 10 syllables. The third and fourth lines also rhyme and should contain 5 to 7 syllables. Here's an example:

> Oh, what should I eat for lunch?
> Hey, I think I have a hunch!
> A soup so creamy,
> It's positively dreamy.
> I love tomato soup a bunch!

Try It!

. . . .
7 to 10 syllables

. . . .
7 to 10 syllables

. . . .
5 to 7 syllables

. . . .
5 to 7 syllables

. . . .
7 to 10 syllables

Haiku

Use this page to write a haiku about a food that you love. A **haiku** is a traditional Japanese poem, and it is three lines long. The whole poem has only 17 syllables. The first and third lines both have 5 syllables, and the second line has 7 syllables. Because they are so short, haiku poems are all about keeping it simple but powerful. Think hard about which words you choose. What are the best descriptive words you can think of? Is your haiku describing the food itself or is it describing the way a certain food makes you feel? Here's an example:

Salty, melted cheese
Golden bread, tangy pickles
My perfect sandwich

Try It!

. . . .

5 syllables

. . . .

7 syllables

. . . .

5 syllables

CHAPTER 4

Answer Key

Chapter 1

TORTILLA SNACK CHIPS

Which tortilla below is divided into 8 equal wedges?

½ of the tortilla:	¼ of the tortilla:	⅜ of the tortilla:

CRANBERRY-ALMOND NO-BAKE ENERGY BITES

Here are other words that describe the appearance and texture of the energy bites and their ingredients:

Oats: Beige, oval, dry, flat

Peanut butter: Brown, gooey, smooth, thick

Sliced almonds: Hard, beige, smooth, oval

Dried cranberries: Sticky, soft, wrinkled

Honey: Sticky, gooey, yellow-orange, thick

Salt: White, rough, solid, cube-shape

Energy bites: Chunky, soft, chewy, sticky

MEATBALLS

1 Answer will depend on how many people are in your family: 1 person (10 meatballs); 2 people (8 meatballs); 3 people (6 meatballs); 4 people (4 meatballs); 5 people (2 meatballs); 6 people (0 meatballs)

2 18 meatballs

3 6 meatballs

BEAN AND CHEESE QUESADILLAS

How many of these rhyming words did you find? Did you think of other rhyming words that aren't on this list?

Mash: bash, cash, dash, gash, hash, rash, sash, slash, smash, splash, trash

Bean: seen, mean, machine, clean, screen, dean, lean, teen, jean, sardine

Cheese: breeze, bees, agrees, sneeze, squeeze, keys, knees, skis

Bake: make, take, break, rake, lake, mistake, shake, steak, flake

BUTTERMILK DROP BISCUITS

2½ cups batter

Chapter 3

WORD SEARCH: PASTA

```
F M I N I U F T K G Z L Z U L Z Z F J M
B V U A B G F Z X H Q O C T I R Y O R N
F S F O A V Q W X Y Y V F T N P V W Z N
P L N A Z W U Z X B G K P J G B S N N S
T V A J R C W C R B W Z H W U P Z V F M
D B Z B Z F I O J Y M X O X I Y O I W N
D U E U U A A P V O D A C E N L O S T N
R C L W F S L L H D M D A C E D C J R I
N A B S C U M Z L W V K B Z B E N I A
F T O G G T B Y L E I P G B A I X W V M
J I W L D S P A G H E T T I V P W H Y G
F N S I A Q M O P K U Z C J O N G E H X
X I W G J P G D J L F I D Y E A C Q R Z
X I H B P Q O O U W I F F P Y G V G Y D
I O X V T G Y D F O A I K D Z U F F H Y
M X R S P X B R G A W W E I H K R K U Y
V T F Z J E H X J D S S H M B E S H I O
G H H W O A N R I G A T O N I I N V F C
P X C U Z Y N N R Q J R F U S I L L I E
G J R Q E G N Y E I I V X D R Z G K V V
```

WORD SEARCH: BREAKFAST

```
G V D J W E U P H G T E K T R Z D O P N
E C T S A M D B K I G J O X T C E I V T
G Q D R F I B A F S A U S A G E B N S L
G W R N F O A T M E A L E V W T X H I S
S H C W L P R D H Y F Q F K P O N Q X N
W Y W K E C N O R U I S B V F A T A K T
I Y W P S X Y G Y O G U R T G S E L N O
K L R D D T L C C A C G O O B T H C P J
Z P J A K M X V H L C Q W X Y T N E V V
N O W R T P D S R S M X M E I E G K R D E
D O U G H N U T S A D N J B Y X P E J A
O K N P D V T P G B B S P K F X N B W J
C X Y P R A Z S E S I N M C D B F N V J
S E G W A M U Y Z U Q N Q O E S S E R U
B O F L L N Y P C O W Y H U O R R W G I
O F T S Z W C N S D A Q J Q X T E E C C
H B R X P K P A I R B K X M W R H A B E
H L D N K N D G K N J F D D H M T I L J
E T Q F F T I A U E W Y F Z N V R O E V
K A K Y W C Z K S E S B B A C O N R M Q
```

WORD SEARCH: KITCHEN TOOLS

```
G H S J H M U Y T G N K G R A T E R S A
W P R C T U W W L R K W Q O C C W G G T
V D K D E W Y T M F X Q I O Q V Y K W
S R C G D Z A H M B N F M V V Y B F K R
E C P X Z C J N O M O I V Y C T K J S C
K G Z Z R G O F Z T Y A F F O G V M E O
J L Y L B B V L S V B W Y E C Z G B H X
S Z A B S O L Z A W D C M I A L X B E B
A M N D R W R M F N O I K S K I L L E T
U I K M L L A S L H D U U W A I J Y C T
C X R O S E H N X H Q E L R H V S V K H
E E W V A X S R X D X H R E X I B Q U V
P R K B C O B G V F U J P Y Q U S Q F R
A K M J N I H L Q J D W M F O G W K Q G
N K T X K E H X E N K K H E K K M P F S
A U O D A L B N U X H O O K F C J X Q M
G E N L I G S P A T U L A G D R Q N N Q
T Q G X L E B T J U N P C F V Q U Z R M
P L S C S O X E I C U F F N Y I A Z G M
F X Y C E V M C S P O O N Z P V B X I A
```

WORD SCRAMBLE: COOKIES

CHOCOLATE CHIP
OATMEAL
SNICKERDOODLE
JAM THUMBPRINT
CHOCOLATE CRINKLE
GINGERBREAD
PEANUT BUTTER
SUGAR COOKIE
SHORTBREAD
MOLASSES
MACAROON
SANDWICH COOKIE

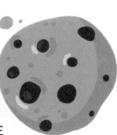

CROSSWORD PUZZLE: DESSERTS!

```
                        C
S T R A W B E R R Y S H O R T C A K E
                        C
                        O
            B R O W N I E        I
                        L        C
        P O U N D C A K E        E
    S                   T        C
    U           L E M O N B A R S
    N       P           C        E
    D       I           H        A
    A P P L E C R I S P          M
    E       O           R
            P           U
            S           P C H E E S E C A K E
            I           C
            C           A
            L           K
            E           E
                        S
```

QUIZ: BUSTING KITCHEN MYTHS

1 **FACT** When you heat water in an open pot, some of the energy that could be raising the temperature of the water escapes with the steam. With the lid on, the water will come to a boil 10 percent faster.

2 **MYTH** Cakes are sturdier than you think, even delicate ones like angel food cake.

3 **MYTH** As long as you cook mushrooms right away, washing them is fine.

4 **MYTH** Stirring your pasta as it cooks prevents sticking, not oil.

5 **MYTH** Searing doesn't keep steaks juicy. In fact, cooking drives off moisture in steaks.

6 **FACT** Strange as it sounds, you really can grow back scallion tops (see page 84)!

QUIZ: FRUIT OR VEGETABLE?

1 Avocados are fruits!
2 Rhubarb is a vegetable!
3 Carrots are vegetables!
4 Apricots are fruits!
5 Lemons are fruits!
6 Olives are fruits!
7 Kale is a vegetable!
8 Bananas are fruits!
9 Raspberries are fruits!
10 Eggplants are fruits!
11 Broccoli is a vegetable!
12 Artichokes are vegetables!

QUIZ: CHEESE!

1 **B.** England
2 **A.** Italy
3 **D.** Greece
4 **C.** France
5 **A.** Mexico
6 **C.** India

QUIZ: FOOD LINGO

1 **SIMMER** To sauté is to cook food in a hot pan with a little butter or oil.

2 **SWEAT** To steam is to cook food in a basket suspended over a pot of simmering water.

3 **POACH** To fry is to cook food in hot oil, such as when making french fries.

4 **BOIL** To broil is to cook food in the oven under the broiler element.

5 **SEAR** To scramble is to stir while cooking food such as eggs.

6 **DICE** To slice is to cut food with a knife into pieces with two flat sides.

7 **FOLD** To peel is to remove the outer skin from fruits and vegetables such as apples and potatoes.

8 **TOAST** To grate is to cut food, such as cheese, into small bits by rubbing it against the holes of a metal grater.

9 **CHOP** To knead is to massage bread or pizza dough into a smooth, round ball.

SPOT THE DIFFERENCES: IN THE TEST KITCHEN

1 Banana's expression
2 The number of cookies
3 Whisk's apron
4 The color of the spatula
5 The color of the mixer bowl
6 The number of legs on the stool
7 The direction of the oven dial
8 Salt versus pepper in Mitsy's shaker
9 Pie versus pizza in the oven
10 The color of the stripes on the cake
11 Something green in Mitsy's pan
12 Bread on Banana's plate

TRIVIA: THE NAME GAME

1 **B.** Tomatoes
2 **C.** Rice
3 **A.** Watermelon
4 **A.** Green onions
5 **C.** Pea
6 **A.** Onions
7 **B.** Beans
8 **A.** Dragon fruit
9 **C.** Seeds
10 **C.** Fruit desserts
11 **A.** Pasta
12 **C.** Raisins
13 **C.** Mushrooms
14 **A.** Edible seaweed
15 **C.** Cremini mushrooms

TRIVIA: WHAT'S IT MADE FROM?

1 **B.** Ground cornmeal
2 **C.** Corn
3 **B.** Fermented soybeans
4 **A.** Melted, browned sugar
5 **C.** Ground-up toasted sesame seeds
6 **A.** Half milk, half cream
7 **B.** Cabbage
8 **C.** Chickpeas
9 **C.** The bark of a tree
10 **A.** Milk
11 **A.** Oil
12 **B.** Cream

TRIVIA: INGREDIENT INVESTIGATION

1 **C.** Citrus fruits
2 **A.** Herbs
3 **C.** Zest
4 **B.** The flower buds
5 **A.** Seeds
6 **B.** Corn
7 **A.** The dried berries of a vine plant
8 **A.** Noodles
9 **A.** Brown rice
10 **C.** Chicken eggs
11 **B.** Chocolate
12 **A.** Mold
13 **C.** Flours
14 **C.** Leaveners
15 **B.** The seed pod of an orchid flower

CHAPTER 5
For Grown-Ups

About This Book

Food and cooking are natural—and fun—ways for kids to learn about many subject areas, from science (biology! chemistry!) to math (fractions! measurement!) to language arts (reading comprehension! vocabulary!) to social studies (food from different regions and cultures!). Cooking engages kids with different interests and abilities, fosters creativity and problem-solving, and creates a whole lot of deliciousness along the way.

Each of the kid-tested and kid-approved recipes in chapter 1 has a "Food for Thought" section. These learning moments focus on a wide range of subject areas and are designed for learners ages 8 to 13. Depending on kids' ages, abilities, and their experience in the kitchen, they may be able to tackle these recipes on their own (or with minimal adult supervision), while other kids might need adult support.

Chapter 2 includes experiments that highlight the important role of science in cooking. Kids will answer questions such as "Why don't oil and water mix?" and "How does whipped cream work?" The hands-on activities in this chapter encourage kids to explore everything from where salt comes from to designing a package that keeps food cold.

Chapter 3 is full of educational, food-focused games, quizzes, and paper-based activities. Some are designed for kids to do on their own, such as Word Searches (pages 100–102) and Design Your Own Food Truck (pages 126-127), while others are fun to play together, such as Mitsy's Silly Stories (pages 106–109) and Would You Rather? Desert Island (page 116).

Visit **ATKkids.com** for hundreds more kid-tested and kid-approved recipes, experiments, activities, and quizzes to bring learning to life in the kitchen.

Food, Cooking, and STEAM

Cooking is an engaging way for kids to learn and apply STEAM content and practice STEAM skills. What is STEAM, you ask? It's more than just the vapor over a pot of boiling water; it's also an acronym for a group of highly integrated subject areas:

Science: The study of the natural world and its physical properties.

Technology: Anything made by humans to solve a problem or meet a need.

Engineering: The process of designing solutions to problems.

Arts: Activities involving skill and imagination, such as visual arts, theater, music, and dance.

Mathematics: The study of numbers, operations, patterns, and shapes.

Science helps us answer questions such as "Why does meat turn brown when I cook it?" and "What does baking soda do to cakes and cookies?" All the tools in your kitchen, from the stove to the whisk to the dish towel, are **technologies**. They've been designed by humans to solve specific problems. **Engineering** results in innovative cooking tools and techniques, new or improved ingredients and recipes, and more. Cooking also involves the creative **arts**, from thinking about how to beautifully plate food or decorate a cake to designing a piece of music inspired by a dish. And **math** is an integral part of cooking and baking. From measuring ingredients to keeping track of time to taking the temperature of food, it's nearly impossible to cook or bake without using math.

As kids work their way through this book, point out when you see them engaging in these STEAM subjects. So often kids (and adults) think of learning as confined to the classroom. Highlighting learning as it's happening in the kitchen draws real-world connections to what kids are learning in school.

Check out Kitchen Classroom (**ATKkids.com/kitchen_classroom**) for additional ideas on how to incorporate STEAM learning into cooking and baking.

Let Kids Take the Lead in the Kitchen

As adults, our instinct is to do whatever we can to ensure that kids' projects succeed, in the kitchen and beyond. This often comes at the expense of letting kids do the work themselves. Think of yourself as their sous chef. You're there to provide encouragement and support when needed and to help with the dangerous bits, of course, but let kids do the lion's share of the tasks. You might be surprised by how much they are capable of when we adults give them the space to try on their own.

Things might not turn out perfectly (and they might not follow the recipe as carefully as you would like), but giving kids ownership over a recipe or experiment builds their confidence in the kitchen and beyond, and instills a sense of pride in their results.

Questions to Inspire Confidence
To foster kids' confidence in the kitchen, here are some questions you might ask while enjoying the (delicious) fruits of their labor.

- **You worked hard! Tell me about how you cooked (or baked) this. What was it like? What steps did you take?**

- **What part was the most challenging for you? How did you get through it?**

- **Would you do anything differently the next time you try this recipe? What would you change?**

These open-ended questions focus on the process of cooking, not the end result. They help kids reflect on their hard work and what they learned, rather than just how their dish turned out.

One Way to Handle "I Don't Know"

If kids respond "I don't know" to all your questions, choose one question and casually respond to their "I don't know" with "If you *did* know, what would you say?" That simple turn of phrase—if you **did** know—frees kids from feeling as if they have to say the "right" answer and lets them say what's on their minds. Deploy this strategy strategically and sparingly—use it too often and it loses its power.

Embrace Failure

There will be times when things don't turn out the way kids had hoped—the pizza burns or the muffins are misshapen. Teaching kids how to persevere through failure and framing failure as part of the learning process helps them move into a growth mindset ("With persistence and learning, I can improve") instead of a fixed mindset ("My ability and intelligence can't change"). Remind kids that just because a recipe didn't turn out the way they expected doesn't mean they aren't a good cook—it means they're still learning. And even imperfect recipes are usually still delicious. Here are our tips for supporting kids when things don't go as planned:

- **Put a timer on sulking.** Tell kids that it's OK and understandable if they're frustrated or sad. You're going to give them 5 minutes to be upset and then you'll work with them to figure out what happened.

- **Share a time when you failed in the kitchen.** Kids don't often get to see grown-ups fail. Telling kids about your own kitchen disappointments helps normalize failure as something that happens to everyone. Emphasize that failure is part of the learning process.

- **Reflect and retrace.** Together, talk through what might have happened. Reverse engineer: Based on the outcome, what do kids think went wrong? (What could have made the pizza burn?) Walk through each step of the recipe and see if kids can identify the problem (Was the oven too hot? Did you bake it for too long?).

- **Don't solve it for them.** Even if *you* know why the cookies turned out flat (they added double the amount of butter!) give kids space to figure it out for themselves. This small act shows kids that you believe they can overcome a challenge on their own.

- **Let kids know you believe in them.** Tell kids that you understand their disappointment but that you know they can succeed if they try again. Reiterate that you're here to support them and help them.

- **Ask if they want to try again.** Once you've talked through what went wrong, provide kids with the opportunity to try again. They don't have to immediately bake another batch of cookies, but encourage kids to use what they've learned and make another attempt in the future.

Failure and Experiments

Experiments for kids often have expected results—when you mix baking soda and an acid, carbon dioxide gas forms. But what if kids' results are different from what's expected? Reassure kids that scientists get surprising experiment results all the time. Sometimes they lead to new discoveries! Scientists also repeat their experiments to see if the same thing happens again. If time allows, have kids reread the instructions and try the experiment again. Do they get the same results? If so, spend some time together trying to figure out what they mean (see Encourage Curiosity, below).

Encourage Curiosity

One of the most powerful things you can do for kids is model and encourage curiosity and wonder. Helping kids carefully observe their world builds observation skills and mindfulness, and helps them make connections.

As you're cooking and eating together, ask questions, listen to kids' responses, and share what you observe. Try using some of the prompts below.

- What do you think will happen when (_____) ?

- What do you notice about (_____) ?

- Why do you think (_____) happened when we (_____) ?

It's OK to Not Know

Kids are naturally curious. The frequency and breadth of their questions can be astounding and sometimes overwhelming. Repeat after us: **It's OK to not know the answer to every question.** Another facet of modeling curiosity is saying, "I don't know, **let's find out**." Showing kids how to find answers, whether through research and reading or exploring the physical world, broadens their knowledge and builds their problem-solving skills.

Table Talk

Conversations around the dinner (or breakfast or lunch) table can be another opportunity for informal learning. As you're enjoying a meal or snack, talk about the flavors, smells, and textures of what you're eating. This not only encourages kids to eat mindfully but also provides opportunities for them to use their observation skills and broaden their vocabulary. Texture Bingo! (pages 72-73) and Bracket: Condiment Madness (page 117) are playful ways for the whole family to talk about food.

It's important to remember that everyone experiences food (and flavor) differently. Our food preferences are highly personal—they're influenced by our genetics and our experiences. Use these conversations as a way to celebrate differences of opinions about food. Remind kids that there isn't one "right" answer about whether something tastes good or not.

Conversation Starters

Mealtime can also be an opportunity for family conversation. Use the prompts below to spark discussion around the table.

- If you could open your own restaurant, what would you call it? What food would you serve?

- What is the first food you can remember eating?

- When is a time you felt proud of something you cooked or baked?

- If you could invent a new gadget or tool to use in the kitchen, what would it be?

- If you could have one superpower while you cook, what would it be?

- Is there a food you changed your mind about (one you didn't like before, but now you do)?

- What's the most challenging thing you've ever cooked or baked?

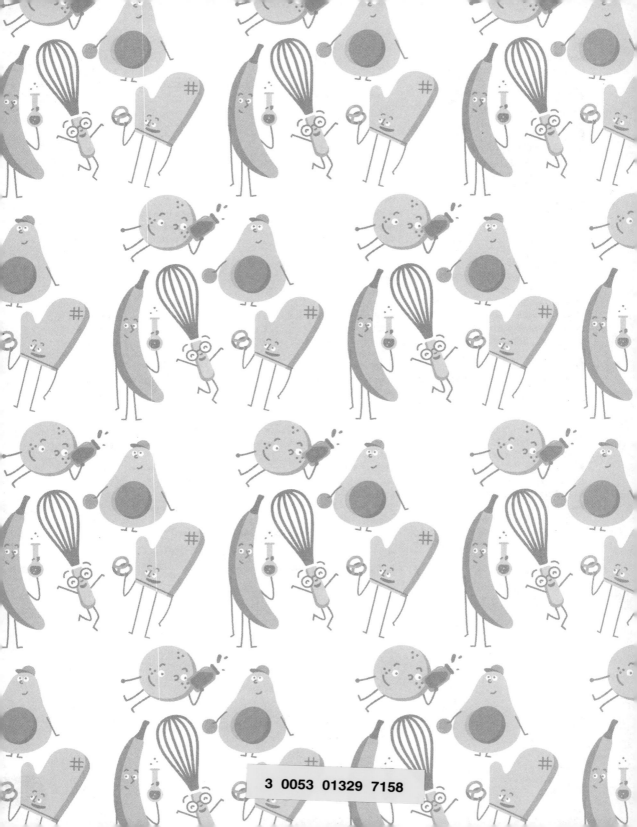